TURNAROUND

To

Love from

Dad xx

First Edition

Paperback: 978-1-0686770-7-6

Disclaimer

This book is based on actual events; however, names, locations, and identifying details have been changed or omitted to protect the privacy of individuals. Any resemblance to actual persons, living or deceased, is purely coincidental.

Contents

Dedicated to the apprentices, men, women and the shareholders who have tirelessly worked for and supported Southbourne Rubber across the years. Your commitment, perseverance, and vision have been the foundation of our success.

“life’s too short to grow old”

"If you're going to miss the bus, miss it running."

1: Crossroads

In early 2016 I stood at a crossroads, my path forward obscured by uncertainty. After seven transformative years at a high-tech material start-up I had been part of a dynamic team that turned a stuttering venture into a global household name. We had shared long hours, hard-earned victories, and the camaraderie that only comes from facing challenges together. But now, my journey there had come to an emotional end. Leaving behind friends, colleagues, and the shared vision we had built was gut-wrenching and for the first time in years I faced an empty calendar, an uncertain future, and the aching void of missing the people and purpose that had defined my days.

To stave off the creeping aimlessness, I picked up a paintbrush and set to decorating a room in my house. It was a task I loathed, yet it offered a distraction from the silence that seemed to amplify the questions in my mind. The days stretched into weeks, and the monotony of painting walls began to mirror the monotony of my new reality. Each brushstroke seemed to echo the same refrain: What now? I hadn't realised how much I craved direction until it was gone.

The turning point came as a text message from a friend. Her company was looking for a project manager, she said. The simplicity of her words felt like a lifeline thrown into turbulent waters. With nothing to lose, I dusted off my CV, polished it as best I could and sent it off. Five days later I found myself sitting across from an interview panel.

The panel—a director and an engineering manager fresh out of the Royal Navy—didn't pull any punches. They grilled me for over an hour and a half, probing every corner of my professional history. Strangely, the absence of desperation gave me a confidence I hadn't felt in years. I answered their questions with a blunt honesty and flippancy that might have seemed cavalier in another context. Somehow, it worked.

Four days later I was called back for a second interview with the then managing director. A week after that I signed on for a six-month contract. It was a short-term role with no guarantees but it felt like a step forward—a way to fill the void and rediscover my footing. The group company was growing fast and my role would focus on readying additional office space for its expansion.

In Waterlooville Hampshire, office space was scarce and when the building opposite their headquarters came up for sale, the company moved quickly to acquire it. My first major assignment was tied to this expansion. As I sat in the meeting room, the excitement of a fresh start gave way to apprehension as one of the directors leaned back in their chair and, with casual nonchalance, dropped a bombshell.

"We've bought a building," they said. "But there's a problem. There's a company in it. We need you to close the company down so we can convert the space into offices."

I paused, unsure if I had misheard. Close a company? My first project wasn't to build or create but to dismantle. I hadn't expected to be tasked with dismantling someone else's livelihood. There was no manual for this, no prior experience to draw on, and the weight of the responsibility settled heavily on my shoulders.

The company occupying the building was a small, struggling rubber manufacturer clinging to life by its fingertips. Its owners had just retired and had long since given up hope; they had done well in the past from the business - retiring with good assets and cash to come. In many ways, to this day, I take my hat off to them. However, they left a dwindling workforce that seemed resigned to the inevitable and machinery relics from the dark ages. My job was to oversee its closure and put the final nail in the coffin. I was to begin the following Monday.

As I walked out of the meeting that day, the gravity of the assignment hit me. This wasn't just a logistical challenge; it was a human one. Lives and livelihoods were intertwined with this failing business, and I couldn't shake the feeling that there was more to the story than I had been told. I didn't know it yet, but this struggling manufacturer was about to become the centre of my professional life. It would challenge me in ways I had never imagined and define the next chapter of my career.

I was about to take my first step into the unknown.

2: Through the Door

For the past seven years, I had been traversing the globe, regularly jetting off to Europe or the U.S. for whirlwind trips lasting between seven and ten days. With young children at home, this relentless travel placed immense pressure on my wife, who carried the weight of family life in my absence. Each trip began with a long-haul flight, followed by a string of one-day hops to visit customers nationwide. Always travelling with just a carry-on, these journeys became a love-hate routine—a blur of airports, hotels, and conference rooms.

A one-hour meeting often translated into two hours of detailed write-ups and the never-ending task of updating Salesforce. The typical itinerary was gruelling: land in Los Angeles, navigate LAX, meet the client the next morning and catch an evening flight to Arizona. After a day there it was off to Dallas, and so the cycle continued. Each trip was a logistical puzzle, stitched together with red-eye flights and rushed connections.

Now, for the first time in years, the prospect of cycling or driving to work for six months felt like a welcome reprieve. Staying physically and mentally grounded was refreshing as it was unfamiliar.

My first day started at 9 a.m., an hour later than the standard company start time. That gave me enough time to meet with the director and review my initial goals. These were presented in broad strokes: assess the situation, identify the key issues, and begin the groundwork for winding down the business. It all seemed straightforward on paper.

Next came the health and safety briefing, an experience. I followed the H&S officer around the unfamiliar building, nodding in vague agreement as they ticked off items on their clipboard. Emergency exits, fire extinguishers, and hazard signage were a blur of acronyms and safety jargon that barely registered. However, the sense of unease creeping into my stomach did stick.

After completing the formalities, it was time to walk through the company's door and meet the employees for the first time.

Born in the rugged expanse of the Falkland Islands, I spent the first decade of my working life immersed in the unforgiving realities of farm life. I thought I had seen it all, the unrelenting wind and rain that seemed to pierce through every layer of clothing, days that stretched from the faintest glow of dawn to well past the fall of night and the relentless toil of managing machinery that always seemed one step away from breaking down entirely. Blood and sweat were my constant companions, especially during lambing season where sometimes a birth was a battle against nature, and emergency caesareans on cows demanded nerves and courage. The work was raw, relentless, unyielding, and at times immensely satisfying, requiring a level of resilience I believed that had prepared me for anything.

Or so I thought.

The moment I stepped inside that building, I was struck by a world unlike anything I had ever known. The heavy, stale air clung to my lungs like it hadn't been refreshed in decades. The fluorescent lights overhead sputtered weakly, casting a dim, lifeless glow that barely pierced the gloom. Shadows clung to the corners, amplifying the oppressive atmosphere.

The smell was the first thing that hit me, a sharp, acrid tang of oil and grease mixed with something indefinably metallic. The scent seemed to seep into your skin, refusing to let go. Beneath it lingered a faint, musty odour of neglect, as if the walls were steeped in exhaustion.

Then came a fierce, unrelenting cacophony of clacking and clanging from machinery that had long since outlived its prime. The noise was deafening, a jarring assault on the senses, each shrill squeal and thunderous crash driving home the stark reality of the place. These machines weren't just old; they were skeletal remnants of a bygone era, their worn-out parts grinding against each other, desperately trying to keep going.

The people inside moved with a weariness that spoke volumes. They worked on a three-day week, their faces etched with a mix of resignation and determination. Shoulders hunched, eyes dulled, their movements lacked the spark of hope but carried the weight of necessity. It was as if the life had been slowly drained from them by the relentless rhythm of the place.

This was no longer the realm of backbreaking physical labour I knew from the farm. It was something darker, more insidious. The building was a monument to decay and decline, where the spirit of industry had been replaced by survival. As I stood there absorbing the scene, I realised this environment would test me in ways I had never imagined, not with physical hardship but with the sheer force of its unyielding bleakness.

Seven people held the company together, each looking like they'd been to hell and back. Their faces told stories of weariness, resignation, and years of struggle. The office was a time capsule from the 1960s, with grey-stained linoleum floors, faded wallpaper, and a musty smell hinting at decades of neglect.

Factory floor May 2016

The technology—or lack of it—was even more shocking. Three ancient computers were shared between Sales and Accounts. Everything else was handwritten on paper or stored on index cards fraying at the edges. A typewriter sat on one desk, clicking and clacking as if it had been plucked straight from a black-and-white film.

Production workstation 2016

And then there was the factory floor. Stepping into the production area felt like stepping onto the set of a period drama. Coated in decades of grime, the machinery wouldn't have looked out of place aboard the Titanic. Black, dirty and deafeningly noisy, it churned and clanked with a begrudging determination.

The air smelled of burnt rubber and oil, and a thick layer of dust clung to every surface. A loud bell rang at an ear-splitting volume as I stood there, taking it all in. Before I could even ask what was happening, the workers dropped what they were doing and bolted from the production floor like their lives depended on it. I stood there bewildered, wondering what I had just walked into.

This wasn't just a struggling company; it was a relic, a living museum of what manufacturing used to be. It was dirty, chaotic, and stuck decades in the past. Looking around I couldn't help but ask myself one simple question:

What on Earth had I let myself in for?

3: History

To understand the company's present, I first delved into its past. The journey began in the early 1970s when the business was established in the nearby village of Southbourne, lending the company its name. By 1973 the company moved to its current location in Waterlooville after the original owner purchased the existing premises. Growth was gradual, driven by careful investment in equipment as customer demand increased.

In the early 1990s the founding owner decided to retire, setting the stage for a transition. After extensive negotiations, a new owner and his financial partner acquired the company in 1995. Over time, day-to-day operations were transferred and the original owner retired fully, leaving the company in new hands.

The new owner brought significant experience in the rubber industry. His career began as a time-and-motion engineer at the Andre Rubber Company, sparking his long-term connection to the field. In 1963 he joined the ITS Rubber Company in Petersfield, a thriving business at its height, employing 300 people. During his tenure he gained valuable management experience as an estimator and work planner, collaborating with sales and marketing teams.

However, ITS's collapse was a harsh lesson in the fragility of businesses. ITS's decline was tied to its reliance on Colston washing machines, a product line moved abroad for cheaper manufacturing.

This left supporting businesses, including ITS, struggling. These challenging years of unemployment shaped the owner's decision to seize the opportunity to acquire a business when it arose.

At the time of the acquisition, the company employed 15 people and benefitted from a strong order book. Its main clients included Marconi, Thorns, military suppliers, and aerospace contractors. The firm specialised in short runs of custom O-rings and grommets, occupying a niche market underserved by competitors. While the premises were modest, they were practical and well-located.

Despite early success, the business began to face challenges. A lack of reinvestment, high staff turnover, and deteriorating working conditions strained the company and its leadership. Over time, these pressures led the ageing managing director and his family to decide to retire and sell.

In April 2016, a local company acquired the business. While this new chapter offered growth opportunities, it also highlighted significant challenges. The ageing infrastructure was increasingly ill-suited to modern demands, requiring substantial updates to keep pace.

4: The First Week

The first week at Southbourne Rubber was a whirlwind—a dense, chaotic mixture of small victories, unresolved issues, and a staggering amount of groundwork to lay. There was no easing into this role; the responsibilities were immediate and urgent, each task pulling in a different direction. The place, with its worn-down equipment, patchy organisation, and faded ambition, desperately needed revitalisation. The path forward required one part triage, one part planning, and much resilience.

The first order of business was an urgent matter: A key quality (DSQR) re-certification for a critical quality programme tied to a major client. The looming deadline in September was non-negotiable yet no clear plan had been laid out for who would attend the required sessions or how the programme would be maintained if certification lapsed. The consequences of failure were stark: losing a key customer that accounted for a significant chunk of revenue. Without re-certification, the trust painstakingly built over the years could crumble in weeks. Meetings were hastily convened to delegate responsibility but the air was thick with apprehension. Every step had to be deliberate, and every decision left little room for error.

Simultaneously, pressing **health and safety concerns** on the shop floor couldn't be ignored. Machinery sat idle with warning signs hastily scrawled in marker, oil pooled in places it shouldn't have been, and safety lines on the floor were invisible. It was not just about meeting compliance standards; it was about ensuring the safety of every individual working there. A mental health list remained unfinished, quotations for necessary safety upgrades languished unsigned, and there was an unspoken urgency to get things moving. This wasn't just a to-do list—it was a matter of fundamental integrity.

Then there were the running costs. In a meeting that stretched on for hours, the company's financial landscape was laid bare: spreadsheets of P&L figures, historical data, and projections that painted a precarious picture. Costs were high, inefficiencies rampant, and the fiscal year was set to roll over at the end of August. Every penny would need scrutiny, every contract reconsideration. Decisions couldn't wait until next week or month; they had to be made now.

Even the email system seemed to embody a state of disarray. The sales inbox, a critical point of contact for customers, had become a source of confusion. Automated "out of office" replies were frustrating clients, and messages were being forwarded and re-forwarded until no one knew who was responsible for responding. It was a logistical nightmare; fixing it required technical adjustments and a clear communication policy.

The shop floor was in a state that could only be described as grim. Dirt clung to every surface, oil streaked across the concrete, and faint safety lines barely whispered the boundaries they once boldly declared. Addressing these issues wasn't merely about appearances but pride, and creating a space where workers felt valued and safe. A plan was sketched to fix leaks, pressure wash the floor, and repaint the lines but it would take time and resources—two things already in short supply.

Even small details reflected the broader chaos. The kitchen, where employees might have found respite, was instead a source of frustration. A kettle perched precariously on a waste bin, sharing an overloaded socket with the microwave and fridge. The water tasted terrible, almost metallic, and a new shelf and filtered water supply were half-finished solutions waiting for completion.

The office space was no better. It was cramped and cluttered, files scattered across multiple rooms like breadcrumbs in a labyrinth. The air conditioning had sputtered to a stop many years ago, leaving the room stifling in the summer heat. My (knee-jerk) plan to tear down panel walls and open the space was ambitious but without new desks, chairs, and maybe even carpet, it would remain just that—a plan.

But amidst all the chaos, there was hope. The First Article Inspection process, long the responsibility of a single overburdened individual, was finally being reassigned. Dropbox was re-evaluated near its storage limit in favour of a more robust system. Customer visits were planned to reconnect with the past and chart a course for the future.

Perhaps the most symbolic moment of the week came with the leaking roof. The work, completed over a year ago, was supposedly under warranty yet here it was again, dripping water onto the company's very foundation. A representative from the facilities company was scheduled to assess the damage. Still, the incident felt like an apt metaphor for everything happening at Southbourne Rubber—a reminder that patchwork fixes could no longer hold.

The first week was messy, exhausting, and riddled with uncertainty. Yet, by the end of it, there was a faint sense of progress. The shop floor had been assessed, emails were untangled, and the groundwork for tackling significant issues was laid. The company's future was precarious and any possibility of a change in the downward trajectory was months, if not years, away.

Monthly Purchase Orders (POs) received. Note the trend line - ever downwards. POs are the lifeblood of any business, and this business was bleeding out.

5: Shutting Down

Having no experience shutting a business down, I did what any sane person would do: read lots of books and scanned the Internet for clues. If only there was a "How to Close a Business Down for Dummies" guide to help me navigate this daunting task.

Shutting down a small business in the UK involves legal, financial, and emotional considerations. Although these steps were never implemented, they were carefully outlined and understood. Below is a detailed guide on the actions required to ensure compliance and fairness throughout the process:

1. Consult with Legal and Financial Professionals

- Solicitors: Seek advice on employment law, contract termination, and managing any potential legal disputes that may arise
- Insolvency Practitioners: If the business is insolvent, engage an insolvency practitioner to navigate liquidation or other insolvency procedures
- Accountants: Obtain guidance on tax obligations, preparation of final accounts, and the distribution of remaining assets

2. Consult with Employees

- Inform Employees: Communicate the decision to close the business transparently, providing clear reasons for the closure
- Collective Consultation: If there are 20 or more employees, you are legally required to consult with employee representatives before initiating redundancies; while not necessary for a smaller workforce, transparency is still critical
- Redundancy Payments: Calculate and promptly pay statutory redundancy payments to all eligible employees
- Support for Employees: Offer practical assistance, such as help with job searching, CV writing, and interview preparation, to support employees through the transition

3. Fulfil Legal Obligations

- Tax Affairs: File final tax returns, settle outstanding taxes, and notify HMRC of the business closure
- Employee Records: Ensure accurate employment, pay, and benefits records are maintained for legal compliance
- Contractual Obligations: Address all outstanding contracts with suppliers, customers, and landlords to avoid breaches or disputes

4. Winding Up the Business

- If Solvent: Consider a Members' Voluntary Liquidation (MVL) to wind up the business while satisfying creditors and distributing remaining assets to shareholders
- If Insolvent: Depending on the business's financial health, explore options such as Creditors' Voluntary Liquidation (CVL) or administration

5. Distribute Remaining Assets

After settling debts and redundancy payments:

- Creditors and Employees: Prioritise paying creditors and fulfilling obligations to employees
- Shareholders: Any remaining assets can then be distributed among shareholders according to their stake in the business

6. Consider Support and Guidance

- Government Resources: For practical advice and support, leverage resources from bodies like the Department for Business, Energy & Industrial Strategy (BEIS) or the Federation of Small Businesses (FSB)
- Employee Assistance: Direct employees to services like Jobcentre Plus for job search help, training opportunities, and financial support

7. Additional Considerations

- Communication Strategy: Develop a clear, consistent communication plan to keep employees, customers, suppliers, and other stakeholders informed
- Financial Planning: Monitor and manage cash flow carefully during the closure to ensure all obligations can be met
- Emotional Support: Recognise the emotional toll on employees and provide support, such as access to counselling services or mental health resources

Shutting down a business is never easy. It requires meticulous planning and execution, empathy, and consideration for the people impacted by the closure. While these steps were theoretical, they represent a comprehensive approach to a challenging process.

6: Tenacity

Tenacity, I'm confident I wasn't born with it. It wasn't something innate, a natural trait I carried from the start. It was something I had to learn, to build, and to earn through experience.

The earliest years of my career didn't demand much of it. Working on a farm, the challenges were physical and predictable—a hard day's work with tangible results. But when I transitioned from technical roles to Sales in the cutthroat world of IT and telecoms, tenacity became not just a skill but a necessity later in life.

At first, it was painful to grow. Rejection wasn't just frequent; it was relentless. Every cold call that ended in a "no," every email ignored and every slammed door chipped away at my confidence. But I soon realised I had two choices: let it crush me or teach me. I chose the latter.

That thick skin didn't develop overnight but it became my greatest weapon once it did. I learned to take rejection as feedback, not failure. Each "no" wasn't the end of the line; it was just another step toward the "yes" I was determined to get. I adapted, refined my approach, and found ways to connect with people who seemed unreachable.

It was down to me if no one else could break into a customer. My colleagues often said, "If you can't get through, no one can." That wasn't just a compliment, it was a challenge—and one I thrived on.

Tenacity is not about persistence. It is about resilience, creativity, and the ability to face rejection with a smile. It's about finding a way forward when every door seems closed and every opportunity seems lost. It is about believing that success is inevitable if you keep pushing, keep trying, and keep innovating.

That same mindset became critical when I found myself at Southbourne Rubber. If I had learned anything from my sales days, it was this: the more complex the challenge, the sweeter the victory. And Southbourne was shaping up to be the biggest challenge of my career.

This six-month project seemed like a slam dunk. The company was already on its last legs, barely held together by ageing equipment and a skeletal staff. Frankly, if I took a two-week holiday, it would crumble to pieces before I returned.

That said, the process wasn't as simple as flipping a switch. Laying off the staff and disposing of the machinery relics wasn't just a logistical task—it was a human one. These seven employees had dedicated years, some a decade, to Southbourne Rubber. Their livelihoods were tied to this place, no matter how outdated and dysfunctional it had become. The thought of walking in one morning and telling them they no longer had jobs wasn't something I could rush into, even if I wanted to.

Then there was the machinery. As antiquated and impractical as it was, these hulking metal beasts had stories. They had once been state-of-the-art, churning out products with precision and efficiency. Now, they were little more than museum pieces, their value reduced to scrap metal. Disposing of them felt symbolic—like erasing the last traces of what Southbourne Rubber had once been.

If I pushed too hard, the entire project could be wrapped up in four months. That might have sounded efficient on paper, but it left no room for nuance, no space to truly understand what this company had been or could still be. I couldn't shake the feeling that there was something here worth salvaging. It was buried under layers of grime, outdated processes and years of neglect, but it was there.

So, I decided to take it slow. Not because I wanted to stretch out the contract but because I wanted to do it right—to give the people and the place the respect they deserved. I tried to understand why this company had survived as long as it had and see if there was a way to honour that legacy.

As the days turned into weeks, that tenacity I'd developed over the years began to kick in. Closing the company was the assignment, but part of me wondered if that was the only option. There was a spark of possibility, faint but persistent, that perhaps Southbourne Rubber didn't need to be a casualty. Perhaps, with the right approach, it could become something more.

But for now, I kept those thoughts to myself. After all, my job wasn't to save the company. It was to close it down. Or so I kept telling myself.

It was time to step back and see what the customers thought of this company. If Southbourne Rubber was to close, I wanted to understand what we were leaving behind—or, at the very least, what had led to its decline.

The sales figures didn't paint a pretty picture. Last year's revenue was just **£365k**, and the trend was unmistakably downward. The order book barely stretched five weeks ahead. After that, well, I had no idea. There was no plan A, let alone a plan B, no pipeline, and only just signs of life.

Still, the best way to understand a company is through its customers, so I decided to track down the top five. It would be helpful if anyone could explain why they still worked with Southbourne Rubber and why others had left. It was time for a road trip.

7: Road Trip

I focused on the top five customers, representing nearly 40% of the turnover. With some planning, I mapped out a route to visit their locations and called each to arrange a meeting. In my experience, securing a meeting is often the most challenging part of the sales journey.

The first call set the tone.

"Hi, I'm Stephen from Southbourne Rubber," I began.

"Who?" came the response.

"Stephen, from Southbourne Rubber," I repeated.

"From where?" they asked again.

And so it went, an endless loop of the same question and the same answer until we were both tired of the repetition. Eventually, we got past the introductions and onto the reason for my call. To my surprise, no one from Southbourne Rubber had ever contacted any of the customers. Half intrigued and half curious, they agreed to meet with me within a timeframe that just about worked for my schedule.

The trip itself felt familiar. I'd done countless road trips like this over the years, meeting new people, understanding their challenges, and learning what they needed. As always, there was the ritual "dance" my old manager used to talk about—the small talk about weather, sports, or whatever else came up while waiting for coffee.

But this time, I had one key question in mind for all of them: *"Why do you do business with Southbourne Rubber?"*

The responses were strikingly consistent.

"The quality is always good. They always deliver on time. And your price is fair. We wish we had more suppliers like you."

“Back of the net.”

I could hardly believe what I was hearing. How could a ramshackle, broken-down SME earn such glowing reviews? The customers clearly valued us highly despite never having visited the site or seen the state of the operation. It was a revelation.

Their feedback was a goldmine, a testament to what the company had been doing right amidst all the chaos. It wasn’t just about the products but about trust, reliability, and delivering what we promised. Now, could I build something on that foundation?

8: Discovery

One ordinary day, after helping clean up yet another oil leak on the shop floor, I found myself in a familiar conversation with the ageing machinery guru I had managed to find to keep everything running. He was one of the last people on Earth who could fix these relics, though his patience was thin. As we discussed the rundown state of the equipment, his advice was blunt: *Get rid of them!*

Walking off the shopfloor, hands slick with oil, I headed to the sink to clean up. As I scrubbed my hands with Swarfega, something on the floor caught my eye—a broken A4 picture frame discarded among other forgotten items. Intrigued, I dried my hands, stooped down, and picked up the frame. It promptly fell apart in my hands, leaving me holding a single, water-stained piece of A4 paper.

Curious, I turned the paper over. What I read stopped me in my tracks: *AIRBUS Approved*. Beneath those words was a small but significant list of parts. Could this be true? Was this company I had inherited once an Airbus-approved supplier?

Adrenaline kicked in, and my priorities for the day shifted entirely. I began digging through every filing cabinet, dusty shelf, and forgotten corner of the office. By the end of the day, I was holding a treasure trove of approvals from some of the biggest names in the aerospace and defence industries: BAE Systems, Rolls-Royce Marine, Leonardo, Thales, Ultra Electronics, and more.

This wasn't just a discovery—it was a revelation. Hidden in the chaos and decay of a struggling business was evidence of a prestigious legacy that might be the key to its future.

The following morning, I gathered all the approvals I'd unearthed and a handful of quality certifications and laid them out neatly on my desk. There were twelve pieces of paper, each more significant than the last. As I stared at them, a thought struck me. I glanced at the blank, magnolia-coloured wall above my desk, then back down at the documents. They deserved more than to be buried in a drawer or stacked on a desk—they needed to be seen.

Determined, I set off for the centre of Waterlooville, intent on finding A4 frames to display the approvals correctly. With Woolworths having shut its doors back in 2008, my next best option was Wilko (now sadly gone too). After searching, I found what I needed and returned to work, eager to implement the plan.

Once back, I carefully placed each approval and certification into its frame, ensuring they were clean and centred. Then, I hung them on the wall above my desk. When the last frame was in place, I stepped back to admire the display.

That's when it hit me. If I genuinely wanted to build an aerospace business, these weren't just documents—they were golden tickets. They were the keys to gaining access to the industry, earning credibility, and laying the foundation for something far more significant than I'd initially imagined.

I stood there for a long moment, looking at those approvals shining proudly on the wall. They stood for a legacy that had been forgotten but not lost. And now, they were my starting point. The path forward suddenly seemed more straightforward, and the potential for what could be achieved felt limitless.

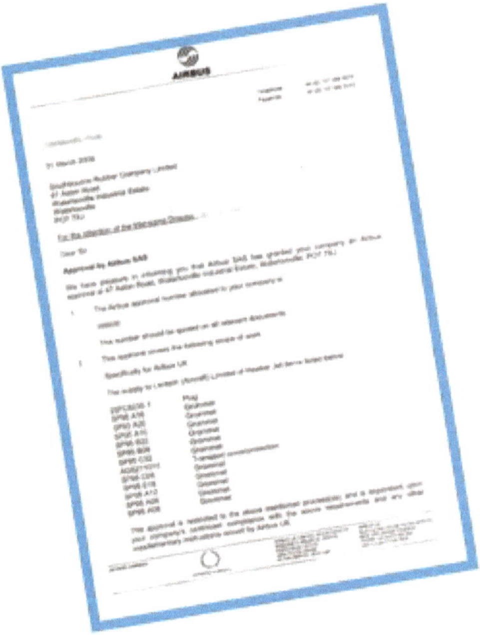

9: The Chairman

The group chairman is a charismatic figure, the kind of man who could command a room with a single glance. He carried himself with a quiet authority underpinned by decades of experience. He had worked for the group since his youth, climbing the ranks not with fanfare but through sheer persistence and an unerring ability to navigate the complex web of group politics. Little about the business's inner workings—or the delicate relationships between the shareholders—escaped his notice. It was his job, after all, to know.

Checks, balances, and smoothing the way. That was the essence of his role. He wasn't flashy or overly domineering, but no one mistook who held the reins. I wasn't entirely sure what he made of me in those first few months. Perhaps I came across as too eager, or maybe my inexperience showed more than I'd hoped. I've often wondered about it; maybe one day, I'll have the nerve to ask him directly.

As luck would have it, we found common ground early on—rugby. A shared passion gave us something to talk about beyond the usual corporate pleasantries. He was as passionate about the game as I was, though our allegiances couldn't have been more different. While he spoke fondly of his local club's triumphs, I wrestled with my enduring loyalty to Leicester Tigers, a team I had supported since a young man. But by then, my devotion was being tested. The Tigers were a shadow of their former selves, a far cry from the glory days when they were a force to be reckoned with.

Still, rugby gave us a starting point, a thread to pull at during those early conversations. And as I would soon discover, there was much more to the chairman than his imposing presence. Beneath the gravitas lay a man of sharp wit and surprising empathy—a combination that would shape my understanding of leadership in ways I hadn't anticipated.

The chairman turned up one afternoon unannounced, as was his way, catching me mid-stride in a blur of paperwork and half-brewed coffee. He had a knack for arriving just when the pressure was mounting, though whether by design or coincidence I was never quite sure. This time he stood there casually, arms crossed, and asked in his measured tone, "So, how are the plans going to close the business?"

This was a good and excellent question—but one I didn't have a straightforward answer to, not for lack of effort but because every day felt like walking a tightrope. Balancing the day-to-day running of the operation while trying not to haemorrhage money was a task that consumed my every waking hour.

"We're keeping the presses running," I began, "but just barely."

The truth was that every press on the shop floor was a ticking time bomb. They were old, cantankerous machines that required constant care to stop them from spitting out oil or grinding to an unceremonious halt. The maintenance cost alone was staggering, and the phrase "extreme measures" barely did it justice. It felt like trying to patch a sinking ship with chewing gum and sheer willpower.

"But we need them operational," I added, as much to myself as to him. "If we stop, it's over. And if we keep going, it's… expensive."

The chairman's expression didn't shift. He nodded as if he'd expected this answer. That was the thing about him—he rarely showed his hand, yet you always felt he understood more than you said.

"Any sane person would have walked away by now," I admitted with a weary laugh. "Left the building, sold the presses for scrap, and called it a day."

He stepped further into the room, his shoes echoing lightly on the worn floor. "And yet here you are," he said, his tone steady. "Why?"

It was a simple question, but it landed like a blow. Why, indeed? There were days when I asked myself the same thing. Days when the numbers didn't add up, suppliers wouldn't pick up the phone, and the faint smell of machine oil seemed to cling to my soul. But there was also something more profound—a stubborn refusal to let it all fall apart on my watch.

"So, what is this business?" he asked suddenly, catching me off guard.

It was another good question I hadn't entirely articulated to myself. I stared at him for a moment before he pressed on.

"Is it the employees?" he asked.

"No," I replied firmly. It wasn't about the people, though I respected their loyalty.

"Is it the machinery?" he continued.

I let out a sharp laugh and gestured toward the shop floor. "Have you seen the broken, dirty, oil-leaking, noisy shite down there? No, it's not the machinery."

"Okay," he said, undeterred. "So what is this business?"

I turned, my eyes settling on the twelve A4 frames I'd recently hung above my desk. The frames were new and bright, but the paper contained within was worn and dulled from years of sunlight, however they still commanded attention. With a deliberate motion, I pointed to them.

"That," I said, "is what this business is. Those certificates represent something most companies can only dream of. You could spend millions of pounds and decades of effort and still not achieve these approvals. This business isn't about presses or people—it's about what those approvals stand for: trust, precision, and capability."

The chairman's gaze shifted to the frames and for the first time I thought I saw a flicker of something in his expression. Respect, maybe.

He nodded slowly. "I see. And do you think they're enough?"

I paused, letting the weight of the question settle. "I think," I said carefully, "that they're a foundation. If we could build on them, this business may still have a chance."

"OK," said the chairman, his tone as calm and composed as ever, though the weight of his following words would hit like a sledgehammer. "I'll tell you what I'd like you to do."

I braced myself.

"In parallel with the plans to close the business down, I want you to prepare something else. There are two months until the next shareholders' meeting. At that meeting, I want you to present a five-year business plan for this company."

I blinked, trying to process what he'd just said.

"Let's see which one wins," he added simply as if he hadn't just doubled—no, tripled—my workload with a single sentence.

He gave me a curt nod, then turned on his heel and strode out of the office, leaving me rooted. My mind was spinning, a whirl of possibilities and panic. Two months. Two months to not only manage the day-to-day chaos of a failing operation and keep the presses from grinding to a halt but now to chart an entirely new course for the company—a course that, if I was being honest, I wasn't sure even existed.

A five-year business plan. A strategy to turn this sinking ship into a flagship.

As I slumped into my chair I took a long breath, running my hand over my head. This wasn't just a challenge; it was an ultimatum. The chairman was testing me, seeing if I could rise to the occasion or crumble under the weight of it all.

My world had officially turned upside down.

I stared at the pile of paperwork on my desk, suddenly feeling like it was just the tip of the iceberg. Beneath it lay uncharted waters—market research, financial projections, operational overhauls, and a thousand decisions that could save or sink the business for good.

This was going to be a *Wilde* ride. No pun intended.

I let out a nervous laugh, already sensing the long nights ahead, the endless cups of coffee, and the mountain of spreadsheets waiting to be built. But there was something else too—something I hadn't felt in a long time.

A spark.

For the first time in months, the future didn't seem like a foregone conclusion. There was a glimmer of possibility, however faint. The chairman had thrown down the gauntlet, and despite the monumental task ahead, I realised a part of me was ready to pick it up.

"Two months," I muttered, grabbing a notepad and pen. "Let's see what I can do."

10: The Five-Year Plan

The company felt like it was running on fumes. The downward trend in revenue, the state of the shop floor and the lack of modern equipment were all symptoms of a deeper problem: the business was dying. It wasn't dramatic or sudden—it was a slow, almost imperceptible decline. And yet, amid the chaos, I discovered a small but vital glimmer of hope.

Buried in a stack of dusty files, I stumbled across several customer approvals. These weren't just routine documents; they were lifelines. These approvals signified trust built over the years and represented opportunities that, if nurtured, could be the foundation of a recovery. It wasn't much, but it was enough to spark a plan.

I began writing the five-year business plan with determination and trepidation. It wasn't just numbers on a page but a manifesto for survival—a way to rally the team, our customers, and myself. The plan was simple: sell more to existing customers and find new ones. But turning that simplicity into a concrete strategy required weeks of deep thought, long nights, and careful analysis.

I liked to think of the plan as stoking a steam train. Without coal, the engine would stall and the train would grind to a halt, stranded on the tracks. With coal it would chug forward, slowly at first, but steadily picking up speed. More coal meant more motion—more sales, customers, and growth. The analogy was perfect: our business was an old train, creaking and groaning but capable of remarkable things if appropriately fuelled.

The first step was to look at where we were. 2016 revenue was **£360k**, reflecting years of stagnation and neglect. The decline had been gradual, almost comfortable in its predictability, but the complacency had to stop. I set an ambitious goal: by 2021, we would reach **£868k** in revenue—a figure that seemed almost unattainable given our current state.

With the target set, I broke the plan into actionable steps. First, I identified our most substantial customers—the ones with approvals already in place. They were loyal but underutilised. I planned to focus on them, deepening relationships, expanding our product offerings, and finding ways to solve their problems. These weren't just transactions; they were partnerships and I wanted to ensure they felt valued and supported.

Next came the search for new customers which felt most daunting. Our reputation was solid but it wasn't enough to rest on our laurels. I spent hours poring over competitor lists, identifying potential industries we hadn't tapped into, and crafting tailored pitches. The idea was to target industries where quality and reliability mattered, sectors that would appreciate the craftsmanship we could offer.

The plan wasn't just about customers in any case. Internally, I outlined investments in people, processes, and equipment. We couldn't grow if the shop floor was unsafe, the team lacked training, or the equipment was held together with duct tape and hope. Every pound we spent needed to be purposeful, driving us closer to our goals.

The months that followed were some of the hardest of my career. Putting the plan into action meant navigating countless obstacles, from reluctant suppliers to skeptical employees who had seen too many promises go unfulfilled. But slowly, the coal started to pile into the furnace.

By 2021, the results were nothing short of staggering. We had not only met but surpassed our ambitious target, achieving a revenue of **£1,141k**—a figure that, at the outset, seemed almost unattainable. The 217% increase in revenue wasn't just a statistical milestone but a resounding validation of our strategy, team, and vision. Every late-night brainstorming session, every difficult decision, every calculated risk—it had all culminated in this extraordinary achievement. And to have reached this point amid a global pandemic, a crisis that brought many businesses to their knees, made the accomplishment even more remarkable. The plan had not just worked; it had flourished against the odds.

By 2024, the upward trajectory had reached an even greater peak, with revenues soaring to an astonishing **£2,711k**. This represented a jaw-dropping **252%** increase from our 2016 baseline. These were not just numbers on a balance sheet—they were a testament to resilience, innovation, and an unyielding commitment to growth. It wasn't merely about surviving; we were thriving, redefining what success looked like for our company and setting new benchmarks for the industry.

Looking back, the business plan wasn't just a roadmap—it was our lifeline, our north star during turbulent times. It imbued the company with a renewed sense of purpose, a belief that we could overcome adversity and emerge more substantial and focused. That steam train analogy had proven prophetic. By 2021, we weren't just moving forward; we were racing ahead, a powerful force that couldn't be slowed down.

The five-year plan had always been designed as a dynamic, rolling framework adaptable to change and prepared to seize new opportunities. And now, as we projected into the next five years, the vision was breathtaking. The momentum we had built was transforming into something more significant—a business tsunami, unstoppable and all-encompassing. The journey wasn't just about achieving targets anymore; it was about redefining the limits of possibility for us and everyone who dared to dream big and commit fully to their vision.

11: Presenting the Plan

It was the quarterly shareholders' meeting and I knew this would be different. I'd spent weeks poring over the five-year business plan, carefully crafting it into something both compelling and accessible. The plan was complete of projections, strategies, and market analysis—pages upon pages of text that could easily overwhelm. So I turned to a method I trusted: visual storytelling.

PowerPoint became my tool of choice, not for a verbose presentation but as a canvas to distil the essence of the plan. Each slide was designed with care—minimal text, bold imagery, and clean charts that told the story at a glance. I wanted the slides to enhance the narrative, not distract from it. I aimed to keep their focus on me as I spoke, guiding them through my vision for the next five years.

When the meeting began I stood before the room, the first slide glowing on the screen behind me. It was an image of the company's logo, flanked by a timeline stretching into the future. I started with a confident tone, explaining the rationale behind the plan—how it wasn't just about growth but sustainable success. I spoke about expanding into new markets, leveraging technology, and improving operational efficiencies.

As I clicked through the slides I could see some heads nodding in agreement. The slides were doing their job: a graph here to illustrate revenue growth, a photo there to emphasise a new product line, and a chart to break down cost-saving measures. It felt smooth, like I was connecting with them.

But the mood shifted as the last slide faded and I opened the floor to questions. The shareholders leaned forward, and their concerns rushed out like a flood.

"What if this doesn't work? How much are we risking here?" one asked, voice sharp.

"This looks good on paper, but can we trust you to make it happen?" another said, looking directly at me.

They weren't questioning the plan's content—it was me—my ability, resolve, and leadership. It was as if they saw me less as the Business Development Manager with a solid strategy and more as an unproven figure standing between them and their financial security.

I answered each question as best I could, pointing back to the data, the benchmarks, and the evidence in the slides. I reminded them of my track record and the time and expertise I had poured into crafting the plan. But it was clear that logic wasn't enough to quell their unease. Their questions weren't just about risks and rewards but about trust.

As the meeting ended, I felt a mix of emotions. I believed in the plan and my ability to deliver it, but I also understood their hesitation. They were being asked to take a leap of faith—not just in business but in me.

It was time for the all-important vote. Two of the shareholders were not in the room. They were beamed in via video conference from the ends of the world—well, not quite, but Chicago and Perth, Australia. The voting got off to a positive start with the founder's backing. The rest followed, although I'm pretty sure some were less than confident.

Walking out of the boardroom, I promised myself I would prove their doubts wrong—not with words or slides, but with results.

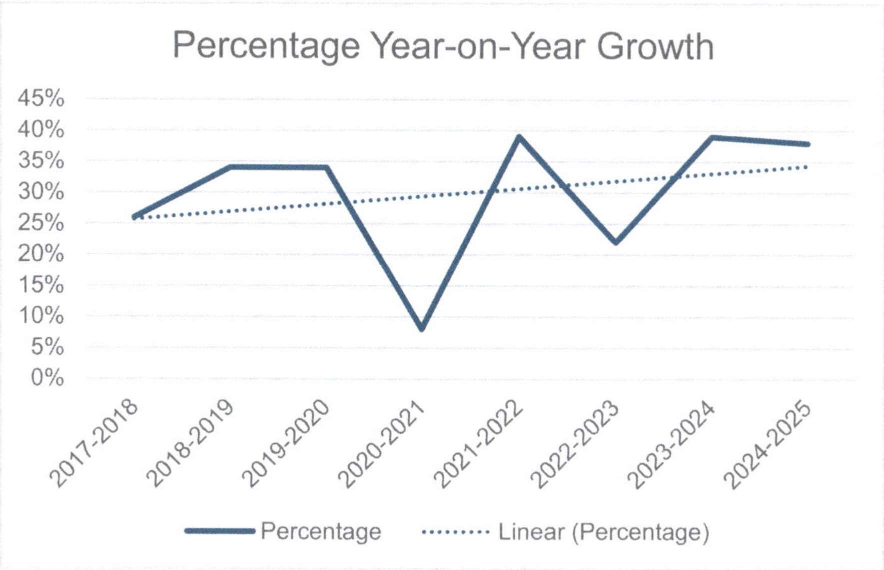

How the plan worked

12: Survival

Make no mistake—the business was teetering on a knife edge. The new owners' directive was clear: the company must not lose money. Breaking even felt like an ambitious goal, and making a profit seemed like a distant dream. But first things first—survival.

There were pressing health and safety issues that couldn't be ignored. Addressing them wasn't optional; it was an immediate and necessary investment. Monies were diverted to fix these glaring gaps, ensuring the team could work in an environment that met at least the basic safety standards.

Then there were the machines. As I've mentioned countless times, their condition was appalling. They consumed vast amounts of cash to keep running. Every day brought a new challenge—breakdowns, oil leaks, and endless repairs. Two power units stopped working entirely, demanding urgent and costly attention.

It felt like a never-ending cycle. Every time one issue was resolved, another demanded time, energy, and money. The business was like a leaky boat, and my job was to plug the holes faster than new ones could appear, all while trying to keep it afloat.

Balancing the books, fixing what was broken, and keeping the team motivated amidst the chaos required constant focus. Every decision felt like a gamble, with no room for error. Survival wasn't just a goal—it was the only option.

Sales were sluggish, and the internal quality of parts was dismal. The wastage levels were staggering, eating away at any potential profit margins. It was clear that something had to change, but finding a way forward wouldn't be easy.

I examined the production process in detail, mapping out each step to identify inefficiencies and pinpoint where things went wrong. It didn't take long to see the cracks—outdated methods, inconsistent practices, and a lack of accountability. Every wasted part was like a knife to the gut, a tangible reminder of money slipping through our fingers.

When I started suggesting changes, the resistance was immediate.

"We've always done it this way," was the standard response.

It didn't matter how glaring the problem was or how simple the solution seemed; the reluctance to try something new was ingrained. It wasn't just skepticism—it was almost a badge of pride, a deep-rooted belief that the old ways were the only ways.

Even proposing a minor tweak was a battle. I suggested slightly adjusting how materials were handled to reduce damage during production. You'd think I'd asked them to reinvent the wheel. The pushback was exhausting, but I knew the business couldn't survive without change.

The challenge wasn't just technical; it was cultural. Shifting attitudes and breaking through the inertia of "we've always done it this way" required persistence, patience, and a willingness to prove, time and again, that change wasn't the enemy—it was the solution.

If the business was going to have a future, the mindset had to evolve. And I was determined to lead that evolution, one small change at a time.

I may have had zero experience in the rubber industry, but I wasn't starting from scratch. I'd worked in factories before and understood the fundamentals of workflows, efficiency, and the basic principles of making a widget. That experience gave me a fresh perspective, and some of the issues I observed were so glaringly obvious that I couldn't believe they hadn't been addressed.

For starters, the shop floor layout was chaotic. Machines were scattered without apparent logic, forcing workers to zigzag across space unnecessarily. Raw materials were piled haphazardly in corners, sometimes blocking access to equipment or tools. Time and energy were being wasted simply moving around. A fundamental reorganisation could save hours of work each week.

Then there was the issue of communication—or lack thereof. Operators worked in silos, often unaware of what the person next to them was doing. There were no clear systems for tracking production or identifying where problems were occurring in real-time. It was like trying to play a football match without knowing the score or even which direction to kick the ball.

Another weak point was the quality control process. Parts were inspected far too late in the production cycle, meaning defective items were only caught after they'd consumed valuable time and resources. A simple introduction of checkpoints earlier in the process could dramatically reduce waste.

When I pointed out these inefficiencies, the responses were predictable. Some shrugged it off. Others gave me that familiar line: "We've always done it this way." But to me, it wasn't just about fixing inefficiencies but about survival.

I wasn't an expert in rubber, but I didn't need to be to recognise that change was essential. The challenge now was convincing the team that these improvements weren't just my ideas—they were the lifelines the business desperately needed.

An old colleague once likened starting a business to trying to get a basketball to bounce while lying motionless on the ground. At first, the ball sits there, inert. You pat it, and it moves slightly. You pat it again, applying more force, and it shifts. It takes significant energy to get the ball moving up and down, much like it takes considerable effort to get a business off the ground.

To get a ball to bounce from the ground, you can push it down into the ground with your feet. The ball springs back up due to Newton's third law which states an equal and opposite reaction for every action. When the ball strikes the ground, the ground pushes back with an equal and opposite force, propelling the ball upward. This interplay of force and motion provides a helpful metaphor for understanding the effort required to get a business moving.

Initially, every decision feels heavy and progress seems painfully slow. Fixing a single machine, reorganising a corner of the workspace, or convincing one person to try something new requires immense effort. But just as a ball, once in motion, begins to bounce with less effort and greater height, so too does a business. Momentum builds. Tasks that once felt arduous become smoother. Efficiency improves, resistance fades, and each push yields more significant results.

Ultimately, it's about perseverance—sticking with the process long enough to see the bounce. Like the ball responding to Newton's third law, the energy and persistence you invest in the business eventually come back to you, multiplied, as progress accelerates.

A stationary ball encompasses potential energy, a form of energy stored within an object due to its position or condition. This energy lies dormant, waiting to be released through an external force. Similarly, Southbourne Rubber embodied potential—an untapped reservoir of possibilities. At this stage, I couldn't fully grasp what that potential might be, but I could sense it was there, much like the ball on the ground, poised to spring into motion if only the right energy was applied.

Just as a ball requires an initial push to convert its potential into kinetic energy, Southbourne Rubber needed a spark—an investment of effort, vision, and direction—to transform its latent promise into tangible results. The challenge lies in identifying where and how to apply that force. Would it be streamlining operations, unlocking new markets, or fostering innovation? The potential was undeniable yet it was shrouded in uncertainty, waiting for the right opportunity to reveal itself.

This realisation brought both excitement and responsibility. The company's untapped energy hinted at opportunities for growth and success but also underscored the weight of action required. Like the ball that can soar if pushed correctly—or stay grounded if neglected—Southbourne Rubber's future depended on finding the right way to harness its potential.

13: Yoda*

Every company should have one. A Yoda, that is. Their wisdom, knowledge, and guidance are instrumental in shaping the lives of the many. At SBR, we had one, albeit he worked on a part-time basis. He probably had other things to do on Tatooine in a galaxy far, far away for the rest of the week. OK, getting back to Earth, his ability to regurgitate a part number was uncanny. He could also tell you what platform it was on, the material it was made from and, most of the time, the commercial value of the part. He was a diamond in the run-down ruins of SBR.

He was the only link left connecting human technical knowledge to the company. If anything happened to him, the company might not have recovered. It was clear that gaining as much technical knowledge from him as possible was paramount. When this became apparent—and business-critical—I sat down with him to discuss the future and his goals. He wanted to move backwards, or maybe it was indeed forward? He wanted to move countries and seek a new life in France.

This revelation hit me like a hammer blow. I knew this was a critical juncture for the business. Try as we might, downloading a lifetime of knowledge in such a niche area was almost impossible. As with the real Yoda, we were sure he used an outside force.

The business in 2016 had regimented holidays: Christmas, one week off; May, one week off; August, two weeks off. Set, non-negotiable. Done and dusted. As luck would have it, that year's May break was the last week in May. I decided it was time to tear down the claustrophobic steel walls that formed mini prison cells across the office.

It was a bold move—one meant to symbolise change and a break from the rigidity of the past—but it was also practical. With the Yoda of SBR potentially leaving, the company needed to reinvent itself, modernise, and create a knowledge-sharing culture. This was not just about the physical environment but also about the mindset: encouraging open collaboration, documentation, and innovation.

Capturing Yoda's knowledge became a mission. Day after day, we tried to document his expertise, recording process, specifications, and every trick of the trade. Still, an element of his insight—the instinctive, almost magical grasp of his craft—seemed irreplaceable. He was more than a knowledge repository; he was the essence of SBR's technical identity.

On holiday Monday I set foot in the empty office, unsure how or what I would do. However, by lunchtime I had the first wall down. Yoda worked on Tuesdays and Wednesdays. I'm not sure whether he'd forgotten it was the holiday week. Anyway, he turned up Tuesday morning, eyebrows raised at the mess and chaos I had created the day before.

I believe he saw his chance to finally tear down the walls of gloom that had surrounded him for years. We both settled into some good old tear-down building work. By Wednesday evening, we had transformed the office into an ample open-plan space—almost modern.

Old office area, May 2016

The staff returned the following Monday, wide-eyed and mouths open. It was as if we had moved buildings. It was precisely the response I was looking for. Onwards and upwards. Where people would scuttle from one tiny room to another, causing delays and slow responses, was replaced by things being gathered and now fully accessible.

The open-plan office brought a new energy. Communication became faster, collaboration more seamless, and morale noticeably lifted. The physical barriers were gone, and with them the metaphorical walls that had stifled innovation and teamwork. Meetings became impromptu huddles around desks instead of formal, drawn-out affairs in cramped rooms. Problems were solved quicker, ideas were shared more freely, and the team began to feel more like a cohesive unit.

Yoda, ever observant, seemed to thrive in this new environment. For all his part-time status, his presence loomed large in the office. The changes had given the company a fresh start and seemed to revitalise him. The open space made his knowledge-sharing sessions more engaging. Gathering around his desk, discussing challenges, and soaking in his wisdom was easier.

The transformation of the office marked the beginning of a new chapter for SBR. The rigid traditions of the past were replaced with flexibility and adaptability. The company was no longer held back by its outdated structures—physical or procedural. It felt like the business had found its footing, ready to advance into a brighter, more connected future.

What all Jedi masters need is a Padawan (apprentice). Unfortunately, I was about the same age as Yoda (896Yrs),

"The walls come tumbling down."

"You can't teach an old dog new tricks" sprang to mind.

In my defence, I was trying to shut down and save a business. Trying to absorb years of technical records, part numbers, and rubber compounds was too much then.

With the arrival of our first apprentice over the next few years, this transfer of knowledge would naturally happen. Watching it was terrific: the student was eager to learn and soak everything up like a sponge, and the teacher went through the gears to stretch and train the apprentice. Yoda seemed to come alive in this role. His passion for the craft reignited as he saw his knowledge take root in a new generation. It was as if the force of his expertise was being passed down, ensuring the survival of the business and its unique capabilities.

SBR's future foundations would be and are built on this transferred knowledge. If anyone ever wonders about the actual value of apprenticeships, look no further.

"Knowledge is power."

Sir Francis Bacon was a philosopher and statesman from 1561 to 1626.

---

*Trademark: Lucasfilm, a subsidiary of Disney, holds trademarks for the name "Yoda" in various categories.

14: Paper Chase

Paper, as we know it, was born in China during the Han Dynasty around 105 CE, credited to a court official named Cai Lun. He pioneered a method that involved mulberry bark, hemp, rags and fishnets, laying the foundation for modern papermaking.

The process spread slowly, reaching the Islamic world by the 8th century and Europe by the 12th. By the time Gutenberg revolutionised printing in the 15th century, paper had become indispensable to human progress. It fuelled revolutions, recorded treaties, carried the words of poets and prophets, and enabled industries to rise centuries later.

However, the paper had its limitations. It could be fragile, flammable, and vulnerable to time. These weaknesses became glaringly evident in the 21st century.

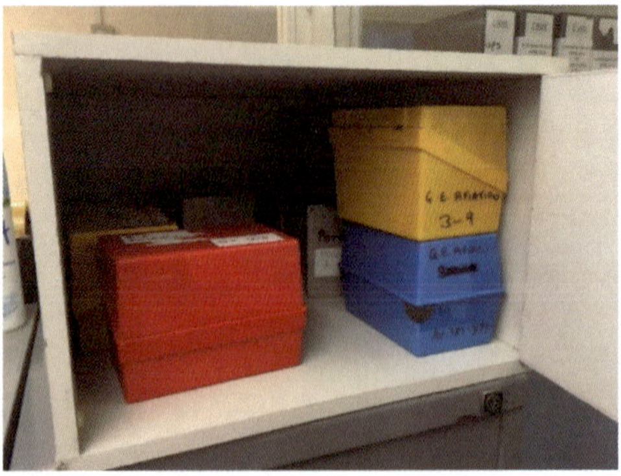

Index cards holding all the data

In the age of digital transformation, where terabytes of data could be backed up in the cloud and accessed in seconds from anywhere in the world, Southbourne Rubber still relied on paper—not as a nostalgic nod to tradition or as a temporary holdover, but as the very backbone of its operations.

The heart of the business pulsed through reams of it. Product sales and customer histories were painstakingly documented on index cards, each holding a story fragment that could only be pieced together by rifling through cabinets. Production, the company's lifeblood, was orchestrated through handwritten A4 sheets scrawled with orders, specifications, and deadlines. The handwriting ranged from elegant cursive to barely legible scrawl, depending on whose pen had recorded the day's needs.

There was a certain charm to it all. The tangible nature of paper—the rustle of it, the weight of a stack of orders in hand—gave the business a visceral quality. Employees knew their way through the labyrinth of folders and files, often relying on memory and intuition to locate what they needed.

Unfortunately, charm couldn't mask the inefficiencies. Running a business on paper in 2016 was increasingly fraught with risk. The system, though functional, was painfully slow. Retrieving a single customer's order history often involved multiple trips to filing cabinets and occasionally heated debates over misplaced cards. Human error, inevitable as it was, compounded the inefficiencies.

But the real danger wasn't inefficiency. It was fire.

SBR's reliance on paper meant the company's entire history—its customer records, product specifications, and production data—was condensed into flammable stacks. Years of painstakingly recorded information would vanish instantly if a fire swept through the office. The business would be left not in a state of disarray but in complete devastation. There would be no backups and no digital archive to restore.

I said, "It would be an almost irreversible journey back to the dark ages."

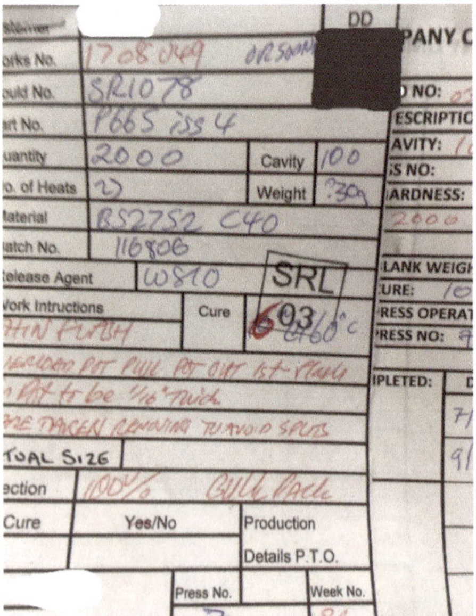

Handwritten production route card

Even beyond fire, paper burns of another kind took their toll. A forgotten folder misplaced on a desk, or an order form stained by a spilled cup of coffee could delay production or frustrate a key client.

By 2016 it was clear that reliance on paper was untenable. Modern businesses demanded agility, transparency, and data security—none of which SBR's paper-based systems could provide.

Southbourne Rubber needed to move forward and, as luck—good or bad, depending on which side of the fence you sat—would have it, the company's parent group was already running SAP.

SAP (Systems, Applications, and Products in Data Processing) is a comprehensive enterprise resource planning (ERP) software that integrates core business processes across departments. It provides real-time data and analytics to improve decision-making and efficiency.

The decision was made to implement SAP at Southbourne Rubber on 1st September 2017. This marked a giant leap for the company—a seismic shift from handwritten scrawls to a digital interface.

The transition, however, was anything but smooth. With little to no training, the team began inputting years of data into SAP. It was a thankless task with challenges, frustrations, and a steep learning curve. The process would take months, even years, to fully integrate, and the path forward was anything but certain.

But for all its teething pains, the shift to SAP signified progress. It was the first step in leaving behind the liabilities of paper and embracing the possibilities of a digital future. Southbourne Rubber was evolving like the medium it had so long relied upon.

15: A New Beginning

In Southbourne Rubber's history, 1972 marked the last time the company invested in new equipment. For over four decades, machinery had carried the weight of production, creaking under the strain of age and wear. When the opportunity to invest in a new press came along it was not just a practical necessity but a symbolic leap forward—a bold declaration of modernity and progress.

The proposed ex-demo 100-tonne vacuum heat press represented more than just an upgrade; it was a paradigm shift. This machine was a marvel of modern engineering designed to revolutionise the manufacture of rubber components. It wasn't merely about replacing the old with the new but redefining production efficiency, quality, and sustainability standards.

The vacuum press was a game-changer for several compelling reasons. Traditional hydraulic presses relied on ambient air to transfer heat and pressure to the moulds. This method was inefficient and prone to defects caused by trapped air bubbles within the rubber. The vacuum press on the other hand, eliminated these inefficiencies by extracting air from the mould before the material was compressed.

By creating a vacuum-sealed environment, the new press ensured uniform heat distribution and pressure application, resulting in:

- Superior Quality: Eliminating air pockets meant fewer defects and a higher yield of perfect parts - this was critical for meeting the stringent quality demands of the aerospace and defence industries, where even the slightest imperfection could lead to failure
- Faster Cycle Times: The vacuum press significantly reduced curing times, enabling the production of more parts in less time - the speed increase alone promised a 150% improvement in cycle efficiency compared to the older machines
- Cost Savings: The new press's precision and reliability resulted in fewer rejected parts and less waste material, directly translating to lower material costs and increased profitability.

Environmental Benefits: The vacuum press consumes less energy and produces less waste, making it a more sustainable option. Its design also minimises the need for harmful chemical release agents, creating a cleaner working environment.

The decision to purchase the press was not taken lightly. Over **£34,000** represented a significant financial commitment for a company still navigating its recovery from years of stagnation. But the numbers were persuasive: the potential savings in operational costs and the expected increase in production capacity far outweighed the upfront expense.

Bringing the new press online was an event. The installation required detailed planning and coordination. Various engineers arrived to oversee the delicate process of positioning the press, ensuring every bolt was tightened and every connection was secure. Once installed, the workforce underwent extensive training to master the machine's advanced features.

For many employees, this was their first experience with such new technology. The excitement was palpable, mixed with a sense of trepidation. Yet, confidence grew as they learned to operate the press and saw its capabilities firsthand, and a sense of pride emerged. They weren't just operating a machine; they were part of a transformation.

Within months, the impact of the new press was undeniable. Production cycles became faster and the quality of output reached unprecedented levels. Customers noticed the improvement, with fewer returns and complaints. The press quickly paid for itself, proving to be an investment in equipment and the company's future.

The acquisition of the 100-tonne vacuum press began a new era for Southbourne Rubber. It demonstrated that even a company with decades of inertia could reinvent itself. The press became a symbol of possibility, a reminder that innovation and progress were not just for startups and tech giants but also for small, resilient businesses willing to take bold steps.

15th June 2017 – Delivery of the first new press

As the hum of the new press became a familiar part of the factory's rhythm, it was clear that this was more than just a machine. It was a promise—a commitment to efficiency, quality, and sustainability. And, most importantly, it was a statement: Southbourne Rubber was moving forward.

The first modern press was far from perfect, but it was all we could afford then. It was key to show and demonstrate what could be achieved with modern technology, and over the coming months it did just that.

16: Funding

In 2018, before the UK shot itself in the foot with Brexit, we were still part of the European Union (EU). Membership had certain advantages, including access to EU funding schemes—a lifeline for small businesses like ours, constantly teetering on a financial knife edge. One scheme caught my attention. It offered to cover 25% of the cost of a new machine, provided the business committed to creating a specific number of full-time jobs.

This was no small opportunity. The machinery we needed was expensive, its cost rivalling our annual profits. Yet it was essential to our survival. Building on the success of our first new press, I wanted to add new machinery. I planned to purchase a double press and a performer. The performer was key to performing the raw materials and ensuring less wastage and better quality. Our current equipment was held together more by hope than bolts, and the maintenance expenses were nearly as high as purchasing a new machine outright. The numbers made it clear: with the latest machinery, we could increase production cycle times by 150%, slash inefficiencies, and finally break free from the cycle of diminishing returns.

But, like most things that sound too good to be true, there was a catch: the paperwork. And oh, what paperwork it was. The application process wasn't just bureaucratic; it was Herculean. Every conceivable aspect of the business had to be documented, scrutinised, and justified. Financial accounts, staffing plans, production schedules, growth projections—each had to be meticulously compiled and cross-referenced. We weren't just asking for funding; we were laying our business bare, exposing its vulnerabilities and potential to the cold judgment of an indifferent panel.

For weeks my evenings disappeared into an abyss of forms, spreadsheets, and supporting documents. When I thought I had completed the final requirement, another email requesting clarification or additional details would arrive. Each submission felt like scaling a new peak, only to discover another summit looming. It was exhausting, maddening and, at times, utterly demoralising.

Yet, through the frustration, I pressed on. The stakes were too high to falter. This wasn't just about securing a subsidy for a machine; it was about safeguarding the future of the business. Without modern equipment, our days would be numbered. With it, we could stabilise, grow, and even thrive. It was the difference between clinging to survival and building a legacy.

Finally, after weeks of relentless effort, I applied. It felt like dropping an anchor after weathering a storm. Now, all I could do was wait and hope that the blood, sweat, and sleepless nights poured into those pages would translate into the support we desperately needed.

As I waited, the numbers haunted me. The cost of maintaining our failing machinery had grown untenable, eating away at what little profit we managed to earn. The prospect of cutting those expenses and boosting efficiency by 150% wasn't just a dream; it was a necessity. I could see it clearly: the gleaming new machine on the factory floor, humming with precision, driving production forward, and giving us the edge we'd long been missing.

Spending **£136k** was sobering, even with the promise of getting 25% of the money back.

Finally the day came. The machinery was already on order—with a six to eight-month lead time, there was little point in waiting for the stars to align. Besides, the grant was based on the invoice for claiming the EU monies. Never has a **£34,000** grant been sweeter. It wasn't just a windfall; it was validation. It was proof that the sleepless nights and endless forms were worth it. The grant marked the first step forward, away from stagnation and towards growth.

I remember the moment vividly: the confirmation email arrived and I stared at the screen, letting the relief wash over me. After months of uncertainty and relentless effort, we had done it. That grant wasn't just money; it was momentum. It was a vote of confidence in our business—a lifeline that signalled the beginning of a new chapter.

The anticipation of the new machinery's arrival added fresh energy to the workplace. It wasn't just a piece of equipment but a symbol of what could be. With it, we could increase production, take on larger orders, and finally compete on a level playing field. The future felt within reach and bright for the first time in years.

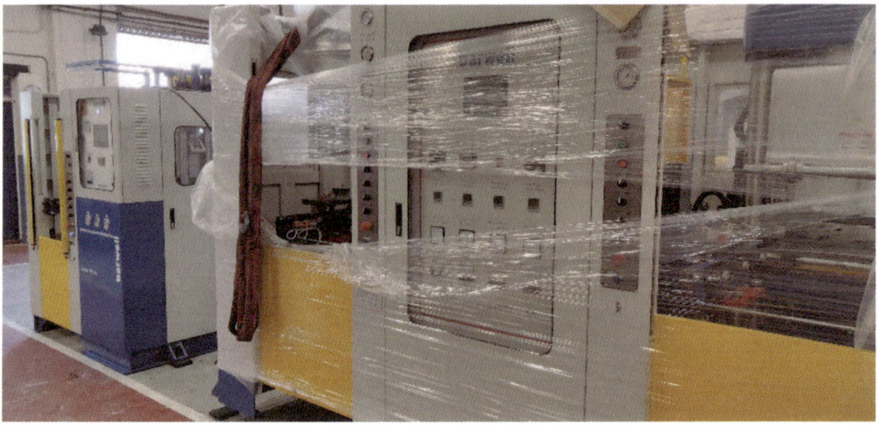

The new double press arrives March 2019

17: Belbin

One of the best companies I have ever worked for used Belbin. Belbin's team-roles theory highlights two paramount attributes everyone brings to a team: their competencies—the specialist knowledge, qualifications and experience that primarily informed their recruitment.

The nine Belbin Team Roles are:

- **Resource Investigator, Teamworker, and Co-ordinator**
    - (the Social roles);
- **Plant, Monitor Evaluator, and Specialist**
    - (the Thinking roles);
- **Shaper, Implementer, and Completer Finisher**
    - (the Action or Task roles).

This company used Belbin to sort potential candidates for the job roles they were seeking. They built the entire company on individuals who had these perceived set roles. The thinking was that no business wants all 'Plants'; otherwise, you would have a group of people who sat around all day throwing up fantastic ideas but wouldn't know how to open a door. Okay, it's a simplification, but correct. This process set the foundation for one of the best companies I have ever worked for.

Remembering this, I was keen to implement this system at SBR. I gathered all the employees and explained the relatively painless 10 to 15 minutes needed to complete the psychometric test. The results were remarkable. The experience was a fantastic team-building event, helping people understand how others thought and why they acted and worked the way they did.

It had been some years since my last Belbin. My job roles had moved from a full-technical role to technical sales, management, and managing director. As with all these learnings and gaining experience, it alters your core competencies. My results showed that my Plant had swapped lead place with Resource Investigator, with my Coordinator in third place, where it had always been.

Team Role	Contribution	Allowable Weaknesses
Plant	Creative, imaginative, free-thinking. Generates ideas and solves difficult problems.	Ignores incidentals. Too pre-occupied to communicate effectively.
Resource Investigator	Outgoing, enthusiastic, communicative. Explores opportunities and develops contacts.	Over-optimistic. Loses interest once initial enthusiasm has passed.
Co-ordinator	Mature, confident, identifies talent. Clarifies goals. Delegates effectively.	Can be seen as manipulative. Offloads own share of the work.

The reasoning for this shift became clear upon reflection. Moving into technical sales required me to develop strong networking skills, make connections, and explore new opportunities—traits central to the Resource Investigator role. The Plant role, characterised by creativity and idea generation, remained vital but was no longer my primary focus. As I progressed into management and eventually to managing director, coordination and delegation became essential, solidifying the coordinator role in its consistent third position. These shifts were a natural evolution driven by the changing demands of my professional journey and the adaptation of my strengths to meet those needs.

The other interesting fact was the first apprentice whom I had worked very closely with, especially in the early years, as detailed earlier. His Belbin profile was a direct echo of my own as if I had cloned my business DNA. This was almost a science experiment with a conclusive result. For those who shrug their shoulders and call it mumbo-jumbo, I would say to you that I have witnessed conclusive proof that:

- Proactive mentoring of a young apprentice can lead to the building of a like-minded individual
- Belbin allows you to track this and detail the results
- You can find out precisely who your team members are

Other psychometric tests could be used in place of Belbin. For example, the **Myers-Briggs Type Indicator (MBTI)** focuses on personality traits and how individuals perceive the world and make decisions. The **DISC Personality Assessment** categorises individuals into four primary behavioural styles: Dominance, Influence, Steadiness, and Conscientiousness. Another is the **StrengthsFinder** assessment, which identifies an individual's top strengths to optimise performance. These tools, like Belbin, offer unique insights into team dynamics and individual behaviours, making them valuable for building effective teams and understanding interpersonal interactions.

18: Continuous Improvement

In December 2013, my former CEO and I embarked on one of the usual "all corners" US business trips. We set off at different times with different agendas and were to meet up in Dallas, TX. I set out from London landing in Dallas where we met and then caught a connecting flight to Lubbock, Texas. I'd taken my usual small carry-on and packed lightly. Having visited Lubbock many times and having been blasted repeatedly by the fierce Texas heat, I'd packed a light business suit and my thinnest cotton shirts. This made sense when leaving home some 18 hours earlier. However, stepping out at Lubbock Preston Smith International Airport and into the open air, the air temperature hit me, to say the least; it was 22F or -5.5C. Bloody freezing.

After a meeting and two nights in Lubbock, we moved on to Minneapolis. I'd forgotten that Minneapolis was in the northern part of the US, and it was winter. Worse still, in December 2013 Minneapolis was struck by a Polar Vortex: a southward shift of the North Polar Vortex brought record-breaking cold temperatures to much of the United States, including Minneapolis.

The temperature drop was staggering. Temperatures plummeted to unprecedented levels, with some areas experiencing temperatures well below zero degrees Fahrenheit for extended periods. The impact was severe: widespread school closures, power outages and an increased demand for heating assistance.

I had packed for a warm-weather business trip, armed with nothing more than a business suit and formal shoes. Just walking down the sidewalks was a joke—dangerous and utterly terrifying. The icy streets were slick and treacherous and the bitter wind cut through every layer. The temperature that day was 4F or -20C. We walked down the road to find some lunch. However, the cold was too great and we dived into the first bar. As we sat there trying to warm up, my boss recounted his sailing metaphor as we sheltered in a bar, taking comfort from a charming bottle of Pinot Noir.

He was a passionate sailor and an exceptionally formidable competitor. He explained that sailing with the wind was effortless—the business was thriving, and everything seemed to align perfectly. Success came easily, momentum carried you forward and progress was almost automatic. But sailing headfirst into a headwind was a different story—it was gruelling and sometimes seemed impossible. The company was faltering, stuck in the doldrums, with no forward motion. Every effort was met with resistance and progress reached a standstill.

However, he emphasised that even sailing at a slight angle—just 10 degrees into a headwind—meant you were still moving forward. It wasn't easy, and it wasn't quick, but it was progress. The business might be challenging but the company wasn't going backwards if you were turning a modest profit.

This metaphor resonated deeply with me. It's a powerful reminder that progress mustn't be perfect, grand, or immediate. It rarely is.

Continuous improvement is about embracing those incremental gains—the minor but meaningful adjustments that accumulate over time and keep you moving forward. It's about resilience—pushing through resistance—and adaptability, finding ways to work within constraints and overcoming challenges. And most importantly, it's about strategy: having a clear sense of direction, even if the journey is slower and more arduous than anticipated.

The true art of continuous improvement lies in appreciating the small wins, the minor adjustments and the enduring effort that ensures steady progress, even when the conditions are challenging.

To me, every month-end and the wait for the P&L (Profit and Loss) accounts to be presented at the board meetings were a point of how far our heads were above water. A loss was a hammer blow; thankfully, there were not that many. Any losses usually came from the aptly named "sore thumbs," as described by the Chairman. A small profit was a lifeline—we could look forward.

Production workstation clear-out November 2018
(see page 15 for the before)

Losses were usually tied to maintenance—lots of it. Breakdowns, lots of them. Machines that should have been the beating heart of production were often the most significant liabilities. Unplanned downtime was like a thief in the night, stealing time, money, and morale. The costs increased quickly: emergency repairs, lost production hours, and the ripple effects on delivery schedules and customer satisfaction. It wasn't just a financial burden but an emotional one too, as the team felt the strain of firefighting problems rather than focusing on growth.

Despite these challenges, even small profits acted as a beacon of hope. They were lifelines that allowed us to regroup, reassess, and refocus. Those moments of progress, however modest, proved that we could navigate through the turbulence and keep moving forward. The key was to identify the root causes of the "sore thumbs" and tackle them with a strategy rooted in continuous improvement.

With little to no money to spend, I was determined to let the staff know we were moving forward, albeit slowly. I focused on small but meaningful changes to signal progress and inspire confidence. I painted a floor, decorated a wall, updated the kitchen—anything to create a visible sense of improvement. These seemingly minor changes were symbolic acts, embedding the employees in the understanding that we were on a journey. Each change was a step forward, however small, reinforcing the idea that we were not stagnant. We were moving ahead together.

New paint and poster March 2020

19: Apprentices

Sales were the key to stopping the business from failing. The numbers didn't lie. Without an uptick in revenue, the company's future would teeter on the edge. We needed someone who could sell and bring energy, resilience, and results. A seasoned salesperson was the obvious choice, but there was one glaring problem: we couldn't afford one without all the demands and expectations of hiring someone experienced.

But I had an idea. It wasn't just about solving the problem I saw before me but about giving something back. Apprenticeships felt like the right path for Southbourne Rubber. They were cost-effective, sure, but more importantly they aligned with my vision for building a company that nurtured potential, not just profits. An apprentice could grow with us, learn on the job, and bring fresh perspectives to our team. Besides, it felt right to invest in the next generation. Still, I couldn't deny that we desperately needed a salesperson.

The challenge was finding the right person. We couldn't afford to get it wrong. I contacted a local agency and explained what I was looking for—not just anyone, but someone with a spark. I told them, "I need someone who plays a sport or has a real passion for something. Someone who knows what it means to commit, to push through challenges, and to work as part of a team."

A week later, six CVs arrived on my desk. I pored over them, looking for that spark, but none stood out. Begrudgingly, I selected two candidates for interviews. Both interviews left me underwhelmed. They were even polite and competent, but there was no drive or hunger. None of them cut the mustard.

Frustrated but undeterred, I went back to the agency. This time, I emphasised—again—what I wanted. "People with passion," I told them, "Passion for a sport, a hobby, anything that shows they've got grit and determination." Send me fewer CVs if you must, but make them count."

Five more CVs arrived. This time, they were better. I sifted through them, weighing my options, and selected two for interviews.

The first candidate was quieter and reserved. He played football for his local team. He was a rough diamond—it was apparent he hadn't had an easy upbringing but he was doing everything he could to move forward, and for that I gave him my fullest respect. When I asked him about football, his face lit up. "It's about support and working together," he admitted, "but there's nothing like the feeling of getting it right on the pitch."

The second candidate walked in with confidence, which immediately grabbed my attention. Standing 6'7", he towered over me. He played rugby he told me, and had been part of his local team since he was young. "I want to play rugby," he said.

"OK," I replied, adding "We don't play rugby here—we make rubber components for aerospace."

The conversation went on; he was interested in sales. My final question was, “Where do you want to find yourself in five years?” Asking most 19-year-olds is like asking an unwritten story what its ending will be.

“I want to play rugby,” he repeated again.

OK, so he has determination and drive. I felt the spark I’d been searching for. Here were two people who understood commitment, who had experienced the ups and downs of striving for something bigger than themselves. They weren’t seasoned salespeople, but they had the raw ingredients.

By the end of the week, I made my choice. The rugby player had an edge I couldn’t ignore. I called him in, offered him the apprenticeship, and told him the truth: “We’re a small company with big ambitions. If you’re willing to work, there’s room for you to grow here.”

He accepted without hesitation. As he shook my hand, I saw an apprentice and a colleague in the making. The road ahead would be challenging but for the first time in a long while, I felt like we had a fighting chance. Yes the company needed sales but it also required belief, and we might have found someone who could bring both.

Little did I know then that my sales apprentice would be the first of many. Over the past seven years, Southbourne Rubber has taken on 14 apprentices. Today, the workforce comprises over 40% former and current apprentices, a testament to the programme's success. These apprentices haven’t just contributed to the company’s growth; they’ve become an integral part of its DNA, shaping the culture and future of the business.

Our commitment to nurturing talent hasn't gone unnoticed. In 2022, Southbourne Rubber was awarded "Best Apprentice Employer of the Year (SME)," a recognition that validated our effort and belief in our apprenticeship programme. The accolades didn't stop there. In 2023, we were named one of the "Top 50 SME Apprenticeship Employers," in 2024, we were highly commended at the Apprenticeship Awards South East.

These awards are more than just trophies on a shelf; they remind us what's possible when a company invests in people. They tell the story of young individuals who walked through our doors unsure of their futures and left equipped with the skills and confidence to excel. They also tell the story of a company that, against the odds, built a sustainable future by selling products and believing in people.

Collecting the PETA Best Apprentice Employer of the Year Award 2022 from the then MP. Penny Mordaunt

Looking back, that first apprentice taught me something invaluable: it's not just about finding someone who can do the job. It's about finding someone who has the heart to grow with you. And in turn, you grow with them. That's what makes all the difference.

UK Top 50 SME Apprenticeship Employer 2023

Highly Commended – Apprenticeship & Skills Awards 2024

Highly Commended – Apprenticeship & Skills Awards 2024

Awarded Gold member of the 5% Club

for investing in apprentices

20: Command Presence

Portsmouth, the historic maritime city on England's south coast, is often described as the birthplace of the Royal Navy. Its docks, steeped in centuries of naval history, have been the stage for some of Britain's most significant maritime achievements. Today, Portsmouth remains the proud home of the Royal Navy, with its legacy shaping the naval force and the city's culture and people.

The foundations of Portsmouth's naval significance were laid during the reign of King Henry VII who established the first dry dock in 1495. By the 16th century, Portsmouth had become the beating heart of England's maritime ambitions. The docks played a pivotal role in constructing and maintaining naval vessels, including HMS Victory, Admiral Lord Nelson's flagship during the Battle of Trafalgar. The Victory, preserved in Portsmouth today, stands as a symbol of Britain's naval dominance and serves as a monument to the bravery and leadership that defined the Royal Navy.

Another iconic ship, the Mary Rose, also calls Portsmouth her final resting place. Henry VIII's favourite warship tragically sank in the Solent in 1545, but it was raised in 1982. It now offers visitors a glimpse into life aboard a Tudor warship. HMS Victory and the Mary Rose embody Portsmouth's role as the cradle of Britain's naval power, where the values, traditions, and sayings of the Royal Navy have influenced generations.

One of the Royal Navy's most enduring traits is the command presence concept. This intangible quality, forged through centuries of naval leadership, is as relevant today as it was during the age of sail. In the Navy, command presence isn't just about rank or authority—it's about inspiring confidence, earning respect, and leading by example.

Command presence is evident in those who can:

- Command Attention: A leader who walks into a room naturally becomes the focus, not by demanding it, but by embodying a calm confidence
- Project Authority: Through their posture, tone of voice, and knowledge, they convey control and competence
- Manage People Effectively: These leaders excel in motivating their teams, maintaining discipline, and fostering loyalty
- Remain Calm Under Pressure: They set the standard in moments of crisis, radiating a sense of steadiness that others can lean on
- Inspire Trust: Their actions align with their words, demonstrating integrity and earning unwavering respect

In Portsmouth, the naval officers and the city's people and businesses have brushed off these traits. Locals admire " command presence, " recognising it as the hallmark of outstanding leadership. Businesses in the area often draw on this naval ethos, fostering cultures of respect, discipline, and responsibility that echo the traditions of the Royal Navy.

One person immediately comes to mind when I think of command presence: the second apprentice I ever took on. From the moment they stepped into the meeting room for their interview, there was something remarkable about them. It wasn't about loud confidence or overpowering charisma but a quiet self-assurance that demanded attention. They carried themselves with a maturity and composure that seemed well beyond their years. They weren't the most vocal candidate in the room, but their words carried weight when they spoke. People instinctively listened, and I knew then that they had potential far beyond the role they were applying for.

They joined Southbourne Rubber as an administrative assistant in 2018. At first, their role was to support the team, learn the ropes of the business, and understand the critical systems that kept our operations running smoothly. However, it didn't take long for their natural aptitude and strong work ethic to shine. Just 18 months later, they were entrusted with running one of the most pivotal departments in the business—a rare achievement for someone so early in their career.

At Southbourne Rubber, administrators aren't just desk workers pushing paper. They are the backbone of the operation, ensuring the production flow is seamless. Their responsibilities include controlling the paperwork that drives production, ensuring compliance, and ensuring that final documents and certifications are sent to customers accurately and on time. It's a demanding role that requires precision, multitasking, and the ability to remain calm under pressure.

In March 2020, the world was turned upside down by the onset of COVID-19. Businesses faced unprecedented challenges, and Southbourne Rubber was no exception. The disruption extended to our workforce, and their boss and mentor—someone they had closely relied upon—left the company. It was a sink-or-swim moment.

What followed was a true testament to their character. Rather than faltering under the pressure, they stepped up and took charge, proving that their command presence wasn't just an impression but a defining trait. They didn't simply keep the department afloat; they made it their own. Systems were streamlined, and they demonstrated leadership that inspired confidence in their team.

Perhaps most impressively, they would go on to train their own apprentice at just 22 years old. Watching them pass on their knowledge and guide someone else through the complexities of the role was a moment of gratification. It was the full-circle realisation of their potential—a quiet confidence turned into undeniable capability.

Their story would not stop there; they would grow further and, within a few short years, become a director in the company.

Their story exemplifies what command presence truly means. It's not about age, title, or experience—it's about stepping into a moment of responsibility and thriving under its weight. From that first interview to leading a key department, their journey remains a reminder that leadership is often recognised not in what someone says but in what they do. This apprentice had a knack for managing situations and people, with maturity beyond their years. They could diffuse tension with a single sentence, motivate their peers without shouting, and make decisions that inspire confidence in others. Watching them grow into their role, I saw firsthand how command presence could not be taught—it was an innate quality honed through experience and self-awareness.

Portsmouth's connection to the Royal Navy is not just historical—it's cultural. The Navy's sayings, values, and practices have woven into the city's fabric. From how businesses are run to how people interact, the lessons of leadership and resilience learned at sea have made their mark on land.

The apprentice with command presence reminded me of the enduring relevance of these qualities. Just as the Navy has thrived for centuries by nurturing leaders who embody these traits, individuals and businesses can also succeed by fostering the same sense of integrity, respect, and confidence.

As I reflect on Portsmouth's history and its role in shaping the Royal Navy, I can't help but feel proud to be part of a tradition that values strong, principled leadership. Whether aboard a ship, in a workshop, or at the helm of a business, command presence remains as vital today as it was in Nelson's time. It is, quite simply, the mark of someone destined to lead.

21: Generations

In 2016, SBR's workforce was heavily biased toward an ageing demographic. The breakdown of employees by generation painted a stark picture:

Baby Boomers (roughly 1946–1964): 13% of the population but represent 29% of SBR's workforce.

Gen X (roughly 1965–1980): 33% of the population and 43% of the workforce.

Millennials (roughly 1981–1996): 36% of the population, but only 29% of the workforce.

Gen Z (1997 onwards): 18% of the population represented 0% of the workforce.

This imbalance highlighted the company's challenges, with a clear overrepresentation of Baby Boomers and Gen X compared to the younger generations. As older employees approached retirement, SBR clearly risked a skills gap without proactive action.

By 2024, the workforce demographics at SBR had shifted significantly, creating a more balanced and sustainable distribution:

Baby Boomers (roughly 1946–1964): Reduced to 18% of the workforce.

Gen X (approximately 1965–1980): Reduced to 25%.

Millennials (roughly 1981–1996): Reduced to 21%.

Gen Z (1997 onwards): Represented 36% of the workforce.

This transformation didn't happen by chance. Recognising the risks an ageing workforce poses, SBR took deliberate steps to attract younger talent. One of the most effective measures was recruiting apprentices.

Apprenticeships became a cornerstone of SBR's workforce strategy. By offering structured training programmes, the company brought in fresh talent and ensured that critical knowledge and skills were passed down from experienced employees to the next generation. Apprenticeships provided a natural way to address the generational imbalance, offering opportunities for young people to build careers in the manufacturing sector while contributing to SBR's success.

These programmes also aligned with SBR's broader goals of fostering innovation and adaptability. Younger employees brought fresh perspectives and a willingness to embrace new technologies, which complemented the experience and expertise of long-standing team members. The intergenerational collaboration strengthened the company's culture and positioned it for long-term success.

By 2024, the positive impact of these efforts was clear. Including a significant proportion of Gen Z employees infused the workforce with energy and innovation. Meanwhile, the balance between generations ensured that institutional knowledge was preserved while fresh ideas continued to flow. SBR's commitment to recruiting apprentices solved an immediate problem and laid the foundation for a sustainable and dynamic future workforce.

22: A Brand's Identity

Logos are more than just symbols. They're the visual handshake of a company, the emblem that greets clients, partners, and employees alike. A logo tells a story—of identity, values, and ambition. For Southbourne Rubber, the existing logo wasn't telling the right story. It was telling the wrong one.

The old logo looked like it had been pulled straight from the 1970s. And it had. Designed decades ago, it might have been modern in its time, but now it feels outdated and uninspired. The bold block lettering and muted colour palette did little to convey the innovative, dynamic company we were becoming. But the element that unsettled me most was the arrow pointing downwards. It didn't sit right with me. To my mind, and perhaps influenced by my amateur understanding of feng shui, that arrow drank all the power and life force out of the business. I couldn't shake the feeling of missed opportunities and the energy draining out of the business every time I looked at it. It was time for a change.

However, a logo is not something you swap out on a whim. It is a cornerstone of a company's identity. Changing it would mean more than a redesign—it would signal a new chapter, a fresh start, and a declaration of intent for the future. I knew the process needed to be deliberate, thoughtful, and collaborative. I wasn't just looking for something pretty; I wanted a logo representing who we were and where we were going.

That is when I came across a local graphic designer whose work caught my eye on Instagram. Her designs were clean, bold, and energetic—exactly what I envisioned for Southbourne Rubber. I reached out, and within a week, we were sitting across from each other, discussing what the logo could be. I shared my thoughts, hopes, and frustrations with the old design. She listened carefully, sketching ideas and asking questions that made me think deeper about what Southbourne Rubber stood for.

"What do you want people to feel when they see the logo?" she asked.

"Confidence," I replied without hesitation. "I want them to see strength, precision, and innovation. I want them to know we are moving forward, not looking back."

The process wasn't quick, nor should it have been. Over several weeks, she sent me drafts and concepts, each inching closer to my vision. Some were too bold, others too generic. But with each iteration, we refined the idea until it felt right. The final design was a triumph. A sleek, modern logo that replaced the downward arrow with an upward motion, symbolising growth and progress. The colours were vibrant yet professional, striking a perfect balance between energy and trustworthiness. It was everything the old logo was not—and everything I wanted it to be.

When revealed, the new logo felt like a breath of fresh air. The team's reaction was immediate and overwhelmingly positive. It didn't just look good; it felt right. It became a source of pride, something we could rally around to symbolise our evolution and ambition.

SBR°
Southbourne Rubber

Updating the logo wasn't just about aesthetics; it was about aligning our external identity with the internal transformation we were undergoing. It was about telling the world, "This is who we are now." Every time I see the new logo on our products, our website, or even a letterhead, it reminds me of the power of reinvention and the importance of getting the details right.

A logo may seem small; it is anything but. It is a beacon for the business, a constant reminder of its mission and values. For Southbourne Rubber, the new logo wasn't just a design update but the start of a new era.

23: Gateway to Excellence

In aerospace, where precision and reliability are not just desired but mandated, the AS9100 standard stands as a beacon of quality. This international benchmark symbolises a commitment to excellence, safety, and continuous improvement for the aviation, space, and defence industries. For companies like Southbourne Rubber, adopting AS9100 was not just an option but a necessity—a gateway to the industry's most critical opportunities.

The story of AS9100 began in the 1990s when the International Aerospace Quality Group (IAQG) recognised a growing need for a universal quality framework. Aerospace manufacturers and suppliers around the globe faced inconsistent standards, leading to inefficiencies and vulnerabilities in a sector where failure is not an option. To address this, the IAQG crafted AS9100, building upon ISO 9001 and tailoring it to the unique challenges of aerospace. It was a monumental step forward, establishing a shared language of quality management across borders.

By mid-2017, it became apparent that AS9100 would become a decisive barrier to entry for companies aspiring to thrive—or even survive—in the aerospace sector. Customers increasingly demanded compliance, viewing it as a litmus test for reliability and credibility. Southbourne Rubber would be locked out of key contracts and opportunities without it. Yet adopting AS9100 wasn't just about ticking boxes; it was about committing to an entirely new standard of excellence.

The decision to pursue AS9100 certification felt like standing at the base of a mountain. The investment of time, resources, and effort was daunting. I estimated the cost of achieving AS9100 would be around **£100,000**—a figure that made me wince every time I thought about it. Much of this would involve hiring a full-time Quality Manager, not just anyone. They had to be aerospace-competent, with the experience and knowledge to guide us through the labyrinth of requirements. Would we even be able to afford them even if we could find someone with the right ability?

The audit itself was another cost that demanded careful consideration. It was a three-day, highly detailed process with an eye-watering price tag of **£8,000**. And that was just for the certification process; the actual expense lay in preparing for it—rewriting our systems, training our staff, and embedding the new culture of quality that AS9100 demanded.

Despite the financial strain, we knew we had to leap. In the early spring of 2018, we hired a full-time Quality Manager. It was a turning point for Southbourne Rubber. Work began immediately, and the scope of the task was immense. Our systems must be entirely rewritten, processes reevaluated, and risks meticulously documented. It wasn't just about creating a paper trail but transforming how we operated at every level.

Months of relentless effort followed. Late nights, endless reviews, and countless revisions became normal. The team's dedication was unwavering, but the journey was far from easy. Yet, as the months passed, the pieces fell into place. The Quality Manager's expertise proved invaluable, guiding us through the intricacies of the standard with precision and focus.

On January the 4th Southbourne Rubber achieved its AS9100 certification. The moment was nothing short of monumental. The certificate represented far more than compliance; it symbolised transformation—a testament to our ability to rise to the challenge and embrace the highest standards of the aerospace industry.

The financial and emotional investment had been significant, but the payoff was undeniable. Gaining AS9100 approval opened doors we had only dreamed of, positioning Southbourne Rubber as a credible and reliable supplier in a competitive market. It was the foundation upon which we built our future, a commitment to excellence that continues to define who we are and what we do.

WORLD CERTIFICATION SERVICES

CERTIFICATE OF REGISTRATION

AS 0162

Single Site

04 January 2019

04 January 2019

03 January 2022

Southbourne Rubber Co. Ltd.

47 Aston Road, Waterlooville, Hampshire, P07 7XJ, United Kingdom

ISO 9001:2015 & AS 9100D

Manufacture and supply of multi purpose rubber seals, grommets, O rings, mouldings, gaskets, fittings.

WORLD CERTIFICATION SERVICES LTD.

04 January 2019

A vital piece of the jigsaw puzzle

24: Busy Fool

Being a busy fool is never good, but in business, it's positively suicidal. It's easy to mistake relentless activity for progress—to believe that simply being busy equates to being productive. But if that busyness isn't strategic or doesn't translate into tangible results, then it's just wasted effort. And in business, wasted effort doesn't just drain time; it drains resources, morale, and, ultimately, money.

I've seen many businesses fall into this trap, but one customer we dealt with at the time was a prime example of what it means to be a busy fool. They would flood us with RFQs (Requests for Quotation) daily—some with multiple lines, others highly complex. Each one required time to process, log, and file. Our team would spend countless hours generating quotes, meticulously ensuring accuracy, chasing answers, and following up. But the worst part? Our win rate was almost non-existent. We weren't winning business no matter how many RFQs we turned around. We were running on a hamster wheel, churning out quotes but getting nowhere.

Looking back, it was madness. We were so caught up in responding that we hadn't stopped to ask the obvious question—was this effort worth it? Or were we just being busy fools?

By mid-2018, with the Farnborough International Airshow on the horizon, I knew we needed to have a direct conversation. The show, held every two years, is one of the most critical events in the aerospace industry—a global stage where businesses showcase their latest innovations, forge new relationships, and strengthen existing ones. This year, I was walking the show with our first apprentice. It was a fantastic opportunity to introduce them to the industry, to show them the scale and potential of aerospace, and, more importantly, to teach them the difference between working smart and simply being busy.

Farnborough International Airshow 2018

From the roar of the air displays to the stands filled with cutting-edge technology, Farnborough was alive with possibilities. But amidst all the spectacle, one meeting stood out as my focus. This customer had a stand at the show, and I had arranged to meet their sales director at precisely 3 PM.

We arrived at their stand on time, ready for what I knew would be a crucial conversation. Their then-sales director was young, bright-eyed, and sharp. He wasn't a fool, which made it even more perplexing that we had been stuck in this endless cycle of futile RFQs. If he was switched on, then why were we both wasting time?

After the usual pleasantries, I didn't waste any time getting to the point.

"Why do you send us so many RFQs?" I asked.

"Why can't you tell us why we're not winning them?"

"Is there a reason we keep quoting but never see any results?"

The questions tumbled out of me, frustration finally boiling over. I expected a well-rehearsed response about competitiveness, market conditions, or internal processes. But to my surprise, his answers were vague. Shrugs. Uncertainty. Admissions that they weren't winning these RFQs either.

And that's when it hit me.

"If you're not winning these RFQs, and we aren't seeing them from other customers, then we're both losing."

We weren't just busy fools—we were mutually busy fools. They were spinning their wheels just as much as we were, pushing out RFQs without any tangible return and clogging up the system with paperwork and processes that led to nothing. It was inefficient at its finest.

At that moment, I saw an opportunity.

"Let's try something for the next six months," I proposed. "We'll drop our price point, but you must do the same. No more unnecessary markups. Let's strip it back and see what happens."

It was a simple agreement, but it was built on logic rather than a blind process. No more markup on markup or inflated pricing, making us uncompetitive before we even started. If we were going to quote, we needed to quote to win.

We shook hands, and from that moment on, everything changed.

That once-lost account skyrocketed. The RFQs that had once felt like a black hole started turning into actual orders. The relationship transformed from a frustrating time drain into a profitable, strategic partnership.

And today? That same customer is now one of our biggest.

The lesson? It's easy to fall into the trap of being a busy fool. To mistake activity for achievement. To be so caught up in the motions that you forget to ask whether they're leading anywhere. But real success doesn't come from just being busy—it comes from being effective.

Being busy is one thing, but being practical—knowing when to challenge inefficiencies, rethink your approach, and turn wasted effort into real opportunity—is what truly drives success. It's not about how much you do but about making sure what you do moves the needle.

25: COVID-19

The end of our financial year on 31st August 2019 marked a significant milestone for Southbourne Rubber. Despite August being a disappointing month that ended in a slight loss, the year had delivered something monumental: we had surpassed the **£815k** sales barrier for the first time in the company's history. That represented a growth of over 34%. It was a moment of triumph, and we were buoyant with optimism. Riding the wave of this achievement, we confidently budgeted for 20% growth the following year. To ensure we kept the growth on track, we included our most expensive capital expenditure for equipment yet—an injection press (detailed in the next chapter).

What could stop us?

Little did we know that an unprecedented global crisis was just around the corner—a pandemic caused by an unknown virus that would threaten lives and challenge the fabric of businesses worldwide.

Our new financial year commenced on September 1st, 2019, infused with the optimism that had defined the prior year. The first quarter performed solidly, staying on budget, and as the months unfolded we continued to hit our financial targets with unwavering consistency. This momentum carried seamlessly into the second quarter and by February 2020 we were six months in, firmly on track and exceeding expectations. The storm brewing around us and the global disruption caused by COVID-19 made these achievements even more remarkable.

Then, our world plunged into chaos. On 23rd March 2020, UK Prime Minister Boris Johnson addressed the nation in a speech that would forever mark that moment in history. The UK was going into lockdown. Businesses were ordered to close, and staff were to be furloughed.

For many, this news brought relief or, at the very least, a sense of clarity in uncertain times. But for Southbourne Rubber, there was little comfort. Due to our contracts with the defence sector, we were deemed an essential business. Closing our doors was not an option. Instead, we faced the daunting challenge of navigating this crisis while remaining operational.

The news landed like a hammer blow. The pandemic had already stretched us thin, and now we had to figure out how to keep the company running in an environment where fear, uncertainty, and risk were omnipresent. The responsibility was immense—not only to our customers and contracts but also to our employees, whose safety and livelihoods depended on us making the right decisions.

We scrambled to adapt. Social distancing measures were quickly implemented on the shop floor. Personal protective equipment became a staple, and sanitisation protocols were enforced rigorously. Communication with employees became more critical than ever as we worked to reassure them while grappling with our uncertainties.

The pandemic tested us in ways we could not have imagined. Each day brought new challenges, from disrupted supply chains to delayed payments from customers facing crises. But despite the adversity, we pressed on. The defence contracts that kept us open became a lifeline, providing enough stability to keep the business afloat.

In the early days of the pandemic, survival became the sole objective. Growth targets were forgotten, and the optimism of the £815k milestone felt like a distant memory. Instead, we focused on adapting, protecting our people, and meeting our obligations as an essential business.

COVID-19 was more than a health crisis—it was a stress test for businesses everywhere. For Southbourne Rubber, it revealed vulnerabilities but also ignited resilience. It taught us that even in the face of a global disaster, there is value in persistence, adaptability, and the determination to keep moving forward.

Easter 2020 arrived, bringing unseasonably fantastic weather that seemed almost ironic given the grim backdrop of a global pandemic. With lockdowns in full force and even a trip to the shops feeling like a military operation, people sought solace in simple pleasures. Flour and other basics were perpetually out of stock as the nation turned to home baking.

Good Friday was a particularly glorious day. The sun shone brightly, the air was warm, and for a few fleeting hours, the world's troubles seemed far away. I decided to make the most of it. The barbecue was fired up by mid-afternoon, and the smell of grilled food filled the garden. With only close family (all within our home "bubble") gathered, laughter and chatter mixed with the music I streamed from my phone to a portable speaker. The drinks flowed, and spirits were high.

As the evening set in, the atmosphere grew even merrier. Then, at around 8 PM, the music suddenly cut out. A moment later, my phone buzzed with an incoming call. I glanced at the screen, perplexed—it wasn't a number I recognised.

"Hello?" I answered, trying to sound composed, though the effects of the beer and wine were evident in my tone.

The voice on the other end said, "Hi, I'm a project manager" from one of our large customers.

"Oh, right. OK," I replied, mentally scrambling to shift gears.

"We need 4,000 gaskets by Sunday," he stated bluntly.

I paused, trying to process what I'd just heard. "You're a day late," I said, laughing nervously, "Everything's closed for Easter."

But the laugh faded quickly as reality hit me. The more significant issue wasn't the timing but the raw materials. "All our suppliers are closed," I explained, trying to steady my voice.

The project manager, clearly desperate, pressed on. "We need them. This is life critical."

There wasn't much to say. "OK," I conceded, "Here's what we'll do. Tomorrow morning—Saturday—we'll head to the office and see what we can manage. No promises, but we'll do our very best."

The call ended, and I stood there, phone in hand, the weight of the situation settling over me. I glanced back at the barbecue and the cheerful scene in the garden. For a brief moment, I considered not saying anything, letting the evening continue uninterrupted. But I knew I couldn't.

"Looks like I've got work tomorrow," I announced, earning a mix of groans and amused disbelief from those around me. The evening was winding down with a flurry of text messages and calls.

The following day, the team—true to their commitment and resilience—gathered at the office. We rifled through inventory, dug through every possible storage space, and brainstormed ways to make it work.

What followed was a testament to ingenuity, teamwork, and sheer determination.

Having arrived at the office around 9 a.m. on Saturday, bleary-eyed but determined. True to their word, the drawings and product requirements were in the inbox, ready for us. The task ahead was daunting—4,000 gaskets by Sunday—but we didn't waste time dwelling on its enormity. Instead, we rolled up our sleeves and got to work.

The first hurdle was materials. We needed a significant quantity of raw materials to get started, and we needed tooling. The office buzzed with activity as we split up the tasks. Phones rang incessantly as we called suppliers, manufacturers, and anyone we thought could help. It wasn't easy—Easter weekend meant most places were closed, and people were reluctant to interrupt their holidays.

By 3PM, after countless calls and negotiations, we had a breakthrough. A material manufacturer agreed to open their facility on Easter Sunday so we could collect what we needed. We quickly arranged for a team member to take a van and pick up the supplies. Meanwhile, the tooling manufacturer agreed to create the required tooling overnight. I volunteered to collect it at the Southampton-Isle of Wight ferry port on Sunday.

The plan was in motion, but the schedule was relentless. Easter Sunday would be one of the busiest and most demanding days ever.

When Sunday morning arrived, the team sprang into action. The van collected the materials as promised and I set off on the drive to Southampton. The streets were eerily quiet—a reminder of the lockdown still gripping the country—but my mind was racing. The timing was everything.

I arrived at the ferry port by lunchtime, picking up the tooling. Standing in an empty port under a bright spring sky, knowing the weight of what we were trying to accomplish, felt surreal. Once I had the tooling safely in hand, I drove back to the office.

The rest of the day was a blur. Machines hummed, and the team worked tirelessly, coordinating every step like a well-oiled machine. It was a race against the clock, but failure was not an option. By the end of the day, we had over 1,000 parts ready for delivery—enough to meet the immediate need.

On Monday morning, a Bank Holiday no less, the first batch was delivered as previously agreed. The relief and satisfaction were palpable, but there was no time to rest. We had 3,000 more gaskets to produce. By Tuesday, the remaining parts had been delivered, fulfilling the order.

What we had accomplished that Easter weekend felt nothing short of a miracle. Moving heaven and earth had become more than an expression— our reality. The team had stepped up, working through holidays, navigating endless obstacles, and turning the impossible into a resounding success. We had a small taste of what the doctors and nurses were going through daily.

As I looked around the office on Tuesday evening, exhaustion mixed with pride. "We did it," I said, and the room broke into smiles and cheers. It was a moment to celebrate the task completed and the resilience, creativity, and sheer determination that had made it possible.

Award for COVID-19 support

Yet, against this backdrop of uncertainty and challenge, our team's resolve and dedication shone brightly, lifting morale and proving our resilience. By the year's end, we celebrated extraordinary growth of 34% again, achieving a significant milestone: surpassing £1 million in revenue for the first time in our history. It was a defining moment, a testament to our collective hard work and determination to thrive against the odds.

The true challenge was still ahead—COVID-19 had more devastation in store for us. Our new financial year began on 1st September 2020, with cautious optimism still lingering from the resilience we'd shown in the early months of the pandemic. However, that optimism quickly gave way to harsh realities. The first quarter proved disastrous, as losses accumulated steadily, month after month. By the second quarter, the situation had only worsened, with no sign of recovery. By February 2021, we found ourselves grappling with a disheartening cycle of financial setbacks six months into the year. Morale was at an all-time low. Each leadership meeting felt like a desperate effort to stay afloat as we brainstormed solutions and tried to inspire confidence. But the relentless figures on the balance sheet painted a grim picture that was impossible to ignore.

At the heart of our struggles was the aerospace sector—specifically MRO (Maintenance, Repair, and Operations), a cornerstone of our business at Southbourne Rubber. MRO is a critical part of the aerospace industry; every aircraft requires regular servicing, and these operations depend on a steady supply of replacement parts. Southbourne Rubber was a key player in providing these components. However, as COVID-19 spread across the globe, commercial air travel came to a standstill. Passenger planes were grounded en-masse as governments imposed travel bans and lockdowns. To put this into perspective, at the peak of the crisis in April 2020, global air traffic fell by nearly 90% compared to pre-pandemic levels. Airlines slashed schedules, mothballed fleets, and postponed or cancelled maintenance cycles. This unprecedented grounding of aircraft had a devastating ripple effect on suppliers like us. Orders dwindled, cash flow dried up, and the demand for our products plummeted.

In hindsight, the downturn was inevitable, but its impact was no less severe. Our reliance on the aerospace sector—particularly MRO—exposed us to a downturn we could not mitigate. The financial strain was relentless, testing the resilience of our team and business model.

There's a well-known saying, "It's darkest before the dawn." At the time, even that faint glimmer of hope felt out of reach. The path forward seemed uncertain, and the weight of the crisis was heavy on us all. Yet, despite the challenges, we knew we had to find a way to navigate the storm.

26: An Injection

Southbourne Rubber had always relied on compression presses for its manufacturing processes. These machines had been the company's backbone for decades, producing countless high-quality rubber components for various industries. However, as dependable as they were, compression presses had inherent limitations that began to constrain our business's growth and potential.

Compression presses operate by pressing raw rubber material between two heated moulds. While effective for many applications, this method is relatively slow and limited in complexity. Each part requires a specific mould, and the process depends on the precise placement of the material and uniform pressure over the mould surface. These limitations made producing intricate or highly detailed parts difficult, if not impossible. Additionally, the cycle times for compression presses were longer, limiting our ability to meet larger orders or more demanding schedules.

Over the years, we encountered opportunities to drive the business forward, particularly in industries requiring high-precision parts, such as aerospace and medical. However, these opportunities came with requirements that our existing technology couldn't meet. The solution was clear: we needed to invest in an injection press.

An injection press fundamentally differs from a compression press's operation and capabilities. Unlike compression moulding, which relies on manually placing material into moulds, injection moulding involves melting the rubber or elastomer material and injecting it into a closed mould at high pressure. This process offers several significant advantages:

- Precision and Complexity: Injection moulding allows for creating highly intricate and detailed parts with tight tolerances - the material is forced into every crevice of the mould, ensuring uniformity and accuracy
- Speed: The cycle times for injection presses are considerably shorter than those of compression presses - this means higher production rates and the ability to take on larger orders without compromising on delivery times
- Efficiency: Injection moulding minimises waste - the exact amount of material required is melted and injected, reducing scrap and improving overall material utilisation
- Scalability: Injection presses are ideal for large production runs - once the mould is designed and set up, the process can run continuously, producing identical parts quickly

However, with these advantages came challenges. Injection presses are far more complex machines than compression presses. They require advanced control systems to regulate temperature, pressure, and injection speed. The moulds are more intricate and expensive, often requiring specialised design and engineering expertise.

Moreover, the cost of acquiring an injection press was substantial. The initial capital investment was daunting, especially for a company like Southbourne Rubber which had continuously operated with a cautious financial strategy. Beyond the machine, we needed to train our team to operate and maintain the press and develop new moulds tailored to this advanced technology.

Despite these challenges, we knew this was a pivotal moment for Southbourne Rubber. The injection press represented more than just a new piece of equipment; it was an opportunity to transform the business, to compete in markets we had previously been excluded from, and to position ourselves as innovators in the rubber manufacturing industry.

As the discussions about this investment unfolded, it became clear that the injection press would require more than just financial resources—it would demand a shift in mindset. We were stepping into a new era that called for boldness, adaptability, and a willingness to embrace complexity for progress.

This chapter in our journey wasn't just about acquiring new technology; it was about redefining what Southbourne Rubber could achieve and setting the stage for a future where the possibilities were limited only by our ambition.

The old floor space had to be cleared, with stock sorted and much discarded as out of date. I wanted the walls and floor painted; this was to be the start of SBR's rebirth. The process of preparation was cathartic. As we stripped away the remnants of the past, it felt like we were making room for a new physical and metaphorical beginning.

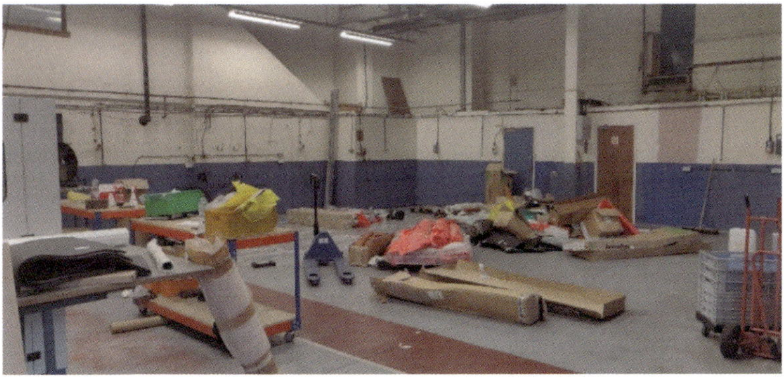

Clearing and sorting material

Preparing the space for the new injection press

The new injection press, 16th June 2020

The press arrived seven months from the point of order, on the 16th of June 2020. It was a momentous day, not just for me but for the entire team. There was a buzz of excitement and anticipation as the machine was carefully unloaded and installed in its newly refurbished home. Two days later, on the 18th of June, we were making production parts. The speed of transition from installation to operation was a testament to the dedication and preparation of our team. It marked the culmination of months of hard work, planning, and investment.

Injection press in action

27: Triple Press

By 2021, Southbourne Rubber had emerged from the tumultuous challenges of COVID-19. 2021 had been one of survival—our growth was a modest 8%, and our financials were teetering on the edge of breakeven. But the key thing was this: we had not made a loss. Many other companies were facing hard times, with some fighting for their very existence. We had weathered the storm, and I was immensely grateful for that.

As the new year began, I sat down to draft the budget for 2021. It was time to move forward, to finally draw a line under one of the legacy issues that had plagued us for years: our old presses. While reliable in their prime, these machines were now an anchor weighing us down. Their inefficiency, high maintenance costs, and excessive energy consumption held us back.

Replacing them had been on my mind for years, but finances always dictated the pace. We could not afford the luxury of top-of-the-line equipment, so we had to make every pound count. After thorough research and negotiation, we settled on a 50-tonne triple press. This wasn't just any press—it was bursting with features, including a vacuum system that promised greater efficiency and precision. The plan was ambitious: to replace nearly 18 ageing presses with a single triple press. It was a bold move, but I was confident it was the right one.

By September, I had secured shareholder approval for the capital expenditure (CapEx), and the order was placed. There was an air of anticipation in the months that followed. This was more than just a purchase; it was a signal of progress, a step into the future.

The last of the old presses, their time was up

The new press arrived on Monday, 22nd March 2021. That same week, we bid farewell to the old presses, clearing and cleaning the area where they had stood for decades. Dismantling those machines was bittersweet. They had served us well, but their time had come.

The old presses removed. Awaiting new press

By Wednesday, the triple press was installed, calibrated, and operational. From the moment it began running, it was clear we had made the right choice. The press was a marvel. It handled tasks with an ease and efficiency that far surpassed its predecessors. The more we asked of it, the more it delivered, never faltering under the demands of production.

A month later, I reviewed the profit and loss (P&L) account when something caught my eye: a discrepancy in our electricity bill. The figures didn't seem right. Curious, I logged into our energy account and cross-referenced the data with our smart meter readings.

The pattern was unmistakable. I could pinpoint the exact days when we decommissioned the old presses and the day we switched the triple press on. The difference was staggering. The old presses had been energy hogs, bleeding us dry with their inefficiency. The triple press, by contrast, was a model of energy efficiency. The savings were so significant that, within a short time, they effectively covered the cost of the new press. From then on, every pound saved on electricity went straight to our bottom line.

It was a revelation. Investing in new machinery wasn't just spending money; it was saving it. The triple press had paid for itself and was now putting hundreds of pounds back into the business every month.

The new press arrives

Looking back, investing in the triple press was a turning point. It reinforced an important lesson: progress requires bold decisions and a willingness to invest in the future. Sometimes, the cost of standing still is far greater than the price of moving forward.

Press awaiting commissioning

The triple press didn't just replace old equipment—it symbolised a new era for Southbourne Rubber. It proved that we could continue to grow, innovate, and thrive with the right tools and mindset.

28: Building Infrastructure

The building that housed Southbourne Rubber (SBR) was a relic of the early 1960s. Like many industrial buildings of its time, it had gone through countless iterations at the hands of previous occupants. Each had made their mark—some improvements, others half-baked fixes that seemed to create more problems than they solved. By the time we inherited it, the building was a patchwork of its past, an unwieldy maze of rooms and corridors that seemed to resist every attempt at modernisation.

The property had one clear advantage: the electrical supply. The building had been blessed with a robust connection to the grid, powerful enough to run our energy-hungry machinery without skipping a beat. But beyond that singular plus point, everything else about the structure felt like a ticking time bomb.

The roof, for example, was a prime example of 1960s construction methods laden with asbestos. It wasn't just on the roof—it lurked in other parts of the building, too. This made even the slightest modifications a health and safety (H&S) nightmare. No matter how minor, every project requires meticulous planning, costly testing, and stringent safety measures.

One of the previous owners had decided to install a sprinkler system which, in theory, was a sensible precaution. In practice, however, it was another disaster waiting to happen. This wasn't an ordinary sprinkler system; it was connected to a 6-inch main water supply.

While the system might have doused a fire effectively, I often wondered what would cause more damage to the building: the fire itself or the flood unleashed by the sprinklers. It was a gamble, and no one wanted to see it play out.

The building's condition mirrored that of the machines on the shop floor—broken, unreliable, and a constant source of frustration. My desk was tucked into a corner of the first-floor mezzanine, an area that could generously be described as makeshift. A bucket sat on the cupboard behind my desk, its practical and pathetic purpose: to catch rainwater dripping through the leaking roof.

Another ongoing concern was the windows. Over half of them were rotting in their frames, some precariously close to falling out altogether. On windy days, you could hear the creaks and rattles, a haunting reminder of their fragility. The carpets were threadbare, worn down by decades of foot traffic, and the kitchen—if you could call it that—was a claustrophobic, poorly ventilated space barely fit for purpose.

Stepping outside the building offered no reprieve. The exterior space was littered with junk—abandoned pallets, rusting metal scraps, and discarded machinery parts that no one had gotten around to dealing with. It was a visual representation of the chaos within, a grim first impression for anyone visiting the site.

Things were bad—there was no sugarcoating it. The building wasn't just outdated; it was actively working against us. Every leak, creak, and patch of rot reminded us how far we had to go. It was a battle not just to maintain the infrastructure but to stop it from completely collapsing around us.

Yet, despite its flaws, the building was ours. It housed our work, our ambitions, and our people. It may have been falling apart at the seams, but it was also the stage upon which we would try to build something better. The challenge wasn't just fixing the building but finding a way to make it work until we could afford to dream of something new.

By 2022, the writing was on the wall, in some places, where peeling paint revealed the decades of neglect underneath. I had always known that something needed to be done about the building's state, but the urgency of the matter came to a head at the start of the New Year.

A very important customer, one whose business we were eager to win, had scheduled a visit. We prepared meticulously for the meeting, ensuring our presentations and proposals were flawless. The discussions went well on the day, better than I hoped. But as the customer left, he left a comment that left a lasting impression.

With surprising candour, he said, "We had nearly turned around and driven back to Derby without even stepping inside the building. It looked so dilapidated that I thought we'd made a mistake coming here."

It was a funny thing, in a way—how the outward appearance of a building could set a tone before a single word was exchanged. But it wasn't funny when I thought about what we had almost lost because of it.

That was the final straw.

April 2022

The building's condition had been holding us back, not just in our operations but in how we were perceived. I knew we had to act decisively, and we had to act now. It wasn't just about patching leaks or replacing a broken window. The entire structure needed a serious overhaul.

The first step was securing the funds. After careful calculations and consultations, I sought a modest mortgage against the building. It wasn't an easy decision—taking on debt is never something to be done lightly—but it was the only way to ensure the future of the business.

By May, we had the green light, and the renovations began.

The scope of the work was extensive. We had decided that the asbestos in the roof had to be carefully over-clad, which required a structural engineer's sign-off. Honestly, nothing was ever simple. This was also a delicate and costly process that required specialist contractors. The new, insulated roof finally stopped the rainwater from entering.

Many of the windows, which were on the verge of collapse, were replaced with modern double-glazed units, improving the building's appearance and significantly reducing heat loss.

December 2022

Inside, the transformation was just as dramatic. The threadbare carpets were ripped up and replaced with durable, easy-to-maintain flooring. The kitchen—once a suffocating, cramped space—was completely gutted, moved, and redesigned into something functional and welcoming. The first-floor mezzanine, where I'd spent years working with a bucket catching drips behind me, was reinforced, updated, and transformed into a production workspace.

Even the outside received attention. The piles of junk were cleared, and the grounds were tidied, creating a clean, professional first impression for visitors.

By the end of the year, the building was almost unrecognisable. Where there had once been rot and decay, there was now a bright, modern facility we could be proud of. The changes were more than just cosmetic—they symbolised the company's direction.

When the renovations were complete, I couldn't help but reflect on our achievements. The process had been stressful, costly, and at times overwhelming. But it had also been necessary. We couldn't continue to grow and compete while being held back by infrastructure stuck in the past.

The first major customer visit after the renovations said it all. As they walked through the doors and toured the facility, there was no hesitation, no second-guessing. They were impressed—not just by the presentations and proposals but by the environment we'd created.

The building was no longer a liability. It was an asset, a reflection of who we were and where we were going. As I stood on the refurbished mezzanine, looking out over the transformed shop floor, I felt something I hadn't felt in a long time—pride.

29: Going Green

2022 marked a turning point for global politics and world events that again forced Southbourne Rubber to tack in choppy waters. The February Russian invasion of Ukraine sent shockwaves through the energy market, causing electricity prices to skyrocket. Overnight, the cost per unit of electricity we were paying had doubled. This hit hard as electricity was our most significant expense outside salaries.

Our energy-hungry machinery, running almost constantly, had always made electricity a significant cost, but this sudden price hike became a major threat to our bottom line. We couldn't afford to wait and hope the market would stabilise. We had to act.

The timing was almost serendipitous. Alongside the ongoing renovations to the building, the chairman and I found ourselves again on the same wavelength about a solution: solar panels. Renewable energy wasn't just a practical move; it was a statement about the kind of business we wanted to be.

I was determined to maximise our roof space and install as many panels as possible. The design was soon completed. On completion, the system would generate up to 50kVA of power on a sunny day—enough to significantly reduce our electricity costs by 30%.

Installing the solar panels wasn't just about cutting costs. It was about future-proofing the business, reducing reliance on external energy suppliers and demonstrating our commitment to sustainability.

Our workforce was young and enthusiastic about the shift toward greener practices. Recycling was already a popular initiative within the company and the solar panel project was met with widespread support.

Solar panels

But we didn't stop there. Around the same time we took another step toward environmental responsibility by becoming members of Ecologi, a platform dedicated to tackling climate change through reforestation and carbon reduction projects.

Since joining, we've committed some of our profits to tree planting and other initiatives through Ecologi. Each month our contribution grows, and so does our forest. It's a small but tangible way to give back to the planet. You can see our progress at https://ecologi.com/southbournerubbercoltd

By mid-2022, the solar panels were installed and the system should have been fully operational. However, due to (yet another) world shortage, this time the humble microchip, our 144 solar panels sat all summer, the sun shining brightly, without producing even a millivolt of electricity. The two inverters that were required were still to be manufactured. Finally, late in December 2022, the panels produced their first power. Watching the meter tick as we generated our power was deeply satisfying proof that we had taken control of one of our most significant expenses while reducing our environmental footprint.

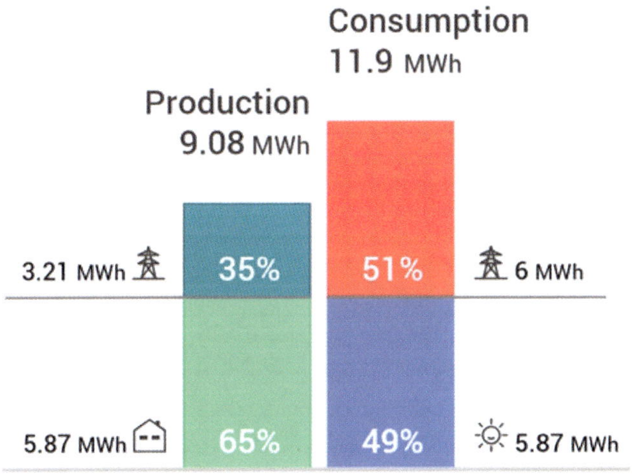

Solar panel production, June 2024

The solar panels and our contributions to Ecologi didn't just save us money; they brought a renewed sense of purpose to the business.

Sustainability wasn't just a buzzword anymore—it was a core part of who we were becoming.

As I walked across the shop floor on a bright sunny day, watching the machines hum along partly powered by the sun, I felt immense satisfaction in what we had achieved. The steps we were taking were not just for the here and now. They laid the groundwork for a cleaner, greener future for Southbourne Rubber and the world around us.

In 2023, Southbourne Rubber decided once again to get ahead of the rest. We decided to determine our carbon footprint. The biggest challenges in determining what your Scope 3 and 4 carbon footprints are:

Scope 3: Complex supply chains, data collection from numerous suppliers and ensuring data accuracy.

Scope 4: Defining avoided emissions, attributing them correctly and verifying claims.

Both scopes face challenges due to a lack of standardisation, resource intensity, and the evolving regulatory landscape. However, we managed to work at it and duly arrived at a figure. We worked with Positive Planet to reduce our carbon footprint. By 2024, we had reduced our footprint by 50% and received a Silver Award for our efforts.

Positive Planet – Silver Award

Our commitment to sustainability aligned perfectly with the growing demands from Tier 1 aerospace companies like Airbus, Boeing and Leonardo. These industry leaders were under intense pressure to address their environmental impact, particularly the criticism of contributing to nearly 8% of global fossil fuel consumption. The call for greener practices resonated throughout the supply chain, urging companies to demonstrate their environmental credentials.

We launched an internal audit to evaluate every aspect of our production processes to meet these demands. From reducing waste to optimising energy efficiency, no stone was left unturned. This effort bolstered our partnerships with key clients and reinforced our reputation as a forward-thinking, environmentally responsible supplier.

As part of this initiative, we began exploring alternative materials and methods to reduce our carbon footprint. Collaboration with clients allowed us to develop solutions aligned with their sustainability goals, creating a win-win scenario for all involved.

By the end of 2023, these efforts had solidified our position as a leader in green manufacturing within the aerospace supply chain. The journey wasn't easy but the results spoke volumes: strengthened client relationships, reduced costs, and a clear path toward a more sustainable future. For Southbourne Rubber, going green wasn't just about compliance and leading the charge in a changing world.

30: Milestones

A milestone is a significant point or event in a journey or process, marking a stage of progress or achievement. It's a moment to pause, celebrate, acknowledge the distance covered, and the determination required to reach that point. For Southbourne Rubber (SBR), the journey is littered with milestones, each representing a triumph over adversity, a bold decision, or a moment of transformation.

2016: The Turning Point

May 2016: The company was sold, a seemingly ordinary business event but one that marked the beginning of a seismic shift for SBR. The new owners, seeking to capitalise on the property rather than the business, decided to close the company. With a turnover of just **£365k**, SBR appeared unremarkable, its potential overlooked by those who now held its future in their hands.

June 2016: A crucial discovery altered the trajectory. SW uncovered several certifications and approvals that elevated the perception of the business. These endorsements hinted at untapped potential, a legacy of quality and reliability that could be leveraged to rewrite the company's story.

August 2016: The chairman issued a dual directive: prepare both a shutdown and five-year business plans. This request highlighted a pivotal choice—conclude the story of SBR or begin a new chapter. The latter would require vision, strategy, and an unwavering belief in the company's potential.

September 2016: The five-year business plan was presented to the shareholders. Despite the uncertainty, the plan was approved and ignited a renewed sense of purpose.

October 2016: SW was appointed General Manager, tasked with overseeing the execution of the five-year plan. It was a vote of confidence in leadership and a commitment to the path ahead.

2017: Laying the Foundation

August 2017: The first tangible signs of growth emerged. Turnover increased to **£479k**. A new press was purchased, signalling a commitment to modernisation and capacity expansion. The first apprentice joined the team, laying the groundwork for a culture of mentorship and growth. SW was promoted to Managing Director.

2018: Momentum Builds

August 2018: Turnover rose to **£605k.** Another press was acquired, reinforcing the company's production capabilities. A second apprentice was brought on board, emphasising a long-term investment in talent development. In May 2018, a new logo was implemented.

2019-2021: Resilience and Growth

August 2019: Turnover reached **£815k.** The business's trajectory was undeniable, driven by a combination of strategic decisions and operational excellence. The first injection press was purchased. Additional apprentices were employed. On 4/1/2019, AS9100 certification was awarded.

August 2020: Despite global challenges, turnover surpassed the £1million mark, closing at **£1,092k.** This milestone was a testament to the company's resilience and adaptability. Injection press #2 and a triple press were purchased.

August 2021: Turnover continued its upward climb to **£1,183k.** The momentum was now a hallmark of SBR's operations. The first apprentice was promoted to Sales Manager and additional apprentices were employed.

2022: Breakthrough Year

August 2022: Turnover surged to **£1,644k.** This remarkable growth reflected the cumulative impact of years of strategic execution, commitment to quality, and investment in people and technology. SBR collected the PETA Best Apprentice Employer of the Year Award 2022 from then-MP Penny Mordaunt.

2023: Leadership in Transition

August 2023: Turnover approached the £2million mark, reaching **£1,998k.** The first and second apprentices, who had grown alongside the company, were promoted to director designates. Their journey from apprentices to future leaders embodied the company's ethos of nurturing talent and rewarding dedication. SBR was recognised as a UK Top 50 SME Apprenticeship Employer 2023. A ZUND digital cutter and a 250t double press were also purchased.

2024: A Vision Realised

August 2024: Turnover soared to **£2,711k**. The first and second apprentices were formally promoted to full directors, a symbolic and practical acknowledgement of their contributions and leadership potential. This milestone culminated in an extraordinary journey for both individuals and the company. SBR was awarded Gold membership in the 5% Club for investing in apprentices.

Business Award 2024

Reflection

Each milestone tells a story of transformation, resilience, and ambition. From the brink of closure to a thriving enterprise, SBR's journey is a testament to the power of vision and the relentless pursuit of excellence. These milestones are not merely points on a timeline; they are the foundation upon which the company continues to build its future, inspiring confidence and hope in all who are part of its story.

31: Leaving a Legacy

Back in 2016, I updated my LinkedIn account with a simple yet ambitious goal: to leave a legacy and build a future foundation for Southbourne Rubber and all its employees. At the time, our turnover was modest—**£365k**. We were a small company with big dreams, navigating a competitive landscape where challenges often outnumber opportunities.

Fast-forward to 2025 and that dream has become reality. With a projected turnover of **£3,500k**, Southbourne Rubber has transformed into a thriving business, achieving nearly tenfold growth in less than a decade. This transformation was not the result of luck but of a deliberate, focused strategy built on resilience, innovation, and the dedication of an extraordinary team.

The journey wasn't easy. In 2016, we were operating out of an ageing facility, relying on outdated machinery, and competing with more prominent players in the market. Our first step was to address these limitations head-on. We invested in modern equipment to improve efficiency and quality, streamlining production processes and reducing waste. Simultaneously, we began diversifying our client base, targeting Tier 1 aerospace companies and other high-value industries that demanded excellence.

It quickly became apparent that to scale we needed to grow, not just our capabilities but also our people. We prioritised recruitment and training, bringing in fresh talent while upskilling our existing workforce. This focus on professional development created a culture of learning and adaptability, enabling us to tackle increasingly complex projects.

Every growth story encounters obstacles, and ours is no exception. From Brexit to the COVID-19 pandemic to the energy crisis triggered by the Russian invasion of Ukraine, external events tested our resilience. But each challenge also presented an opportunity.

Brexit forced us to rethink our supply chain and deepen relationships with European and global partners. The pandemic accelerated our adoption of digital technologies, streamlining communication and project management. The energy crisis pushed us to innovate, leading to installing solar panels and implementing other green initiatives that reduced costs and positioned us as a forward-thinking company.

These experiences taught us the value of agility. Instead of reacting to change, we embraced it, using adversity as a catalyst for growth.

The turning point came in 2020 when we redefined our mission: to be a supplier and a partner to our clients, delivering solutions that exceeded expectations. This shift in mindset unlocked new opportunities. By collaborating closely with Tier 1 aerospace companies like Airbus and Boeing, we became integral to their supply chains, valued for our technical expertise and commitment to quality.

Our focus on sustainability further differentiated us. As aerospace giants faced mounting pressure to reduce their environmental impact, our green initiatives—from solar energy to waste reduction to exploring bio-based materials—aligned perfectly with their goals. This alignment strengthened existing relationships and attracted new clients who shared our vision for a greener future.

As I reflect on the past nine years, the numbers tell one part of the story, but the real legacy lies in what those numbers represent. They represent apprentices who have started their careers and helped build the foundations of Southbourne Rubber, the other jobs created, and the lives improved. They represent innovation and a commitment to excellence. They represent a company that rose to every challenge and emerged stronger.

In 2025, Southbourne Rubber will be more than just a business; it will be a community. Our employees are not just workers but stakeholders in a shared vision. Our clients are customers and partners in a journey toward innovation and sustainability. Our impact extends beyond our walls, contributing to a greener, more equitable world.

Our foundation is strong, but the journey doesn't end here. Those who come after me will write the next chapter, guided by the principles and values that have brought us this far. I hope they will continue to dream big, take bold steps, and remember that the accurate measure of success is not just in what we achieve but in the legacy we leave behind.

As I step back and hand over the reins to the next generation of leaders, I do so with immense pride and gratitude. Southbourne Rubber's story proves that anything is possible with vision, determination, and a team that believes in the mission. Here's to the future and the legacy we've created together.

SBR

Southbourne Rubber

Southbourne Rubber is also known as SBR. Incidentally, SBR also stands for **S**tyrene-**B**utadiene **R**ubber.

32: Gallery

Old machinery

Old presses and power unit - May 2016

Scrap metal - June 2016

Rebuilding the old roller shutter door

The old office space, cleared and transformed

The far lefthand corner where my desk used to sit and the rain came pouring in.

Digital cutting room

Local street artists brightening up the offices.

Old tooling area - February 2022

New temperature-controlled store - May 2022

One of the many box offices before the walls came down.

33: About the Author

Stephen Wilde is a fifth-generation Falkland Islander who now lives in Hampshire, England. He has humble roots and a strong work ethic. He spent his formative years on a farm.

For the first decade of his professional life, he continued to toil in the agricultural sector. Later, he embarked on further education, navigating self-improvement through perseverance. He adapted to the changing industry tides by transitioning into electronics, IT, and telecoms.

However, the tumultuous waves of the 2008 economic crash led to unemployment. During this period of uncertainty, he lasted 11 long months. Until fate intervened, he would traverse the globe and contribute to an exciting new material and product.

In 2016, he was at another crossroads when he seized the chance to shift gears and embrace a new role as managing director. Now, he has authored a book(s)…

If you would like to read more about the author, this short book details Stephen's 'lucky' existence after five generations of disease, disasters, two world wars and the toss of a coin.

Lucky to survive five generations of
disease, disasters, two world wars
and the toss of a coin.
LUCKY
STEPHEN WILDE

Printed in Great Britain
by Amazon

58353362R00091